EDUCATORS

SUPPORTING

EDUCATORS

Margery B. Ginsberg

Joseph F. Johnson Jr.

Cerylle A. Moffett

Association for Supervision
and Curriculum Development

Alexandria, Virginia USA

A Guide to Organizing School Support Teams

Association for Supervision and Curriculum Development
1250 N. Pitt Street • Alexandria, Virginia 22314-1453
Telephone: 1-800-933-2723 or 703-549-9110 • Fax: 703-299-8631
Web site: http://www.ascd.org • E-mail: member@ascd.org

Gene R. Carter, *Executive Director*
Michelle Terry, *Assistant Executive Director, Program Development*
Ronald S. Brandt, *Assistant Executive Director*
Nancy Modrak, *Director of Publishing*
John O'Neil, *Acquisitions Editor*
Julie Houtz, *Managing Editor of Books*
Jo Ann Irick Jones, *Senior Associate Editor*
Karen Peck, *Proofreader*
Gary Bloom, *Director, Editorial, Design, and Production Services*
Karen Monaco, *Senior Designer*
Tracey A. Smith, *Production Coordinator*
Dina Murray, *Production Assistant*
Cindy Stock, *Desktop Publisher*

Printed in the United States of America.

ASCD Stock No.: 197016
ASCD member price: $17.95; nonmember price: $21.95
s8/97

Library of Congress Cataloging-in-Publication Data

Ginsberg, Margery B.
Educators supporting educators : a guide to organizing school support teams / Margery B. Ginsberg, Joseph F. Johnson, Jr., and Cerylle A. Moffett.
    p.   cm.
Includes bibliographical references (p.).
ISBN 0-87120-281-6 (pbk.)
1. School support teams—United States. 2. Educators—United States—Professional relationships. 3. Teachers—In-service training—United States. 4. Mentoring in education—United States.
I. Johnson, Joseph F., Jr. II. Moffett, Cerylle A.   III. Title.
LB2822.82.G55   1997
371.102—dc21   97-23099
                                                    CIP

01 00 99 98 97   5 4 3 2 1

Educators Supporting Educators:
A Guide to Organizing School Support Teams

Acknowledgments   v

Foreword   vii

1. School Support Teams and Schoolwide Programs: A Window of Opportunity   1

2. Making It Happen   15

3. Designing Professional Development for School Support Teams   27

4. Questions and Answers   57

Bibliography   61

Appendixes
A: Title I Legislative Summary   63
B: Overheads: Effective Schoolwide Programs   70
C: State-Level Letter of Introduction   73
D: Regional- or District-Level Letter of Introduction   75
E: Nomination Form for School Support Team Members   77
F: Response Form for Participation on a School Support Team   78
G: Coordinating the Work of School Support Teams Diagram   79
H: Title I Schoolwide Program Planning School Support Team Request Form   80
I: Letter of Introduction from a School Support Team Coordinator   81
J: Campus Profile Information Form   82
K: Program Description Guide   88
L: Overheads: Brief Lecture on Improving America's Schools Act, Section 1117   89
M: "Getting Reform Right: What Works and What Doesn't"   94
N: Recommendations from the Texas School Support Team Pilot Initiative   102
O: School Reform Study Group Dialogue Guide   104
P: Needs Assessment Study Group Dialogue Guide   122
Q: "Site-Based Facilitation of Empowered Schools: Complexities and Issues for Staff Developers"   146

About the Authors   151

Acknowledgments

This book is the result of the leadership, talent, and generosity of many people. In this regard, we are especially grateful to the leadership of B. J. Gibson, Anita Villarreal, and Anne Neel at the Texas Education Agency. Their vision and insight undergird the integrity of this initiative. We would also like to thank the 12 pilot year school support team coordinators, their teams, and the schools they visited. Their experiences and stories continue to inspire. In addition, we would like to express our gratitude to the regional school support team coordinators at Texas's 20 education service centers. They understand the meaning of change in more ways than we can count, and they demonstrate the power of perseverance, resourcefulness, and caring—for one another as well as for the schools and districts they serve. For the numerous conversations, perspectives, and materials shared by the staff of all of the technical assistance centers—and especially the Region E Technical Assistance Center that was located at RMC Research in Denver—we would like to convey a special thank you. They have catalyzed a legacy of resources and personnel dedicated to creating the conditions for schools to courageously question themselves on behalf of all students. We are also deeply grateful to our editor, Jo Ann Jones, for her consistent encouragement, flexibility, and intellectual support.

This book is lovingly dedicated to our families. Our families are the people with whom we practice the world we would like to create. They inspire our allegiance to learning.

Margery B. Ginsberg
Joseph F. Johnson Jr.
Cerylle A. Moffett

Foreword

"It is impossible to overestimate the amount of training, development, and support that school teams need as they begin a collaborative change effort. It has become very clear that the key role in serious change is that of a facilitator."[1]

Why This Book?

In 1995 the United States Congress initiated a transformation in the way we have traditionally worked with children in high-poverty schools. Guided by the vision of a collaborative, schoolwide approach to comprehensive instructional reform in high-poverty schools, Congress reauthorized the federally funded Chapter 1 compensatory education program as a bold, new Title I program under the Improving America's Schools Act (IASA). Rather

than addressing the problem of low student achievement through pull-out remedial programs, the new Title I legislation seeks to eliminate dual standards by requiring that the standards for all children in schools eligible for Title I assistance be the same challenging standards that states develop for every student in every school. Thus, with a stroke of the pen, Public Law 103-382 has reframed the question, "How do we fix the child?" to "How do we improve the entire school so that we work well with all students?"

The schoolwide approach to change is consistent with current research. It gives educators at the local school site the flexibility to

- Reconfigure the school day,
- Increase collaboration among the instructional staff,
- Study new and promising practices to teaching and learning,
- Control school resources,
- Combine federal funds to initiate innovative practices that meet the needs of all students, and

---

[1]E. R. Saxl, with M. B. Miles and A. Lieberman, (1989), *Assisting Change in Education,* (New York: Center for Policy Research; Seattle: University of Washington; Alexandria, Va.: Association for Supervision and Curriculum Development).

• Be released from unnecessarily restrictive mandates related to such issues as student groupings, minutes of instruction, and detailed curriculum sequences.

Most important, the Title I schoolwide concept gives teachers and administrators the opportunity to imagine what might work best for their own students in their own school—with the assistance of external facilitators known as "school support teams." The legislation suggests that school support teams (SSTs) be composed of skilled teachers and administrators, pupil services administrators, pupil services personnel, and distinguished educators from K–12 and postsecondary education who have had experience with successful school improvement initiatives.

As we began to conceptualize systems of school support teams and prepare them for their work with schools, we became intrigued with the potential of the concept of teams of "external change agents" who could serve as facilitators, coaches, mentors, and resource providers in schools experiencing instructional challenges. As our experience broadened, we became convinced that this approach had the potential to transform not only Title I schools, but any school wishing to elevate the quality of curriculum and instruction.

The book is an outgrowth of our experience providing professional development to more than 2,000 school support team members over a three-year period, our involvement with the Texas School Support Team Pilot Initiative, and our involvement conceptualizing the potential of this opportunity with several state and regional SST coordinators. We encourage you to use the ideas and resources to conceptualize old and new approaches to supporting school improvement in your own settings.

How Is the Book Organized?

This book is designed as a resource for educators in any setting: a school, a district, a regional service center or educational cooperative, a state education agency, or an institution of higher learning. We have focused on information that educators seeking to implement the concept of school support teams would find most useful. The practical guidelines and examples we provide are undergirded by a strong foundation in educational research in such areas as school change, adult motivation, cultural diversity, constructivist learning, and professional development.

Chapter 1 provides an overview of the schoolwide approach to change and the role of school support teams. A case study illustrates what the process might look like in a school. There is also a detailed description of what we have learned over time in concert with 20 education service centers throughout Texas.

Chapter 2 provides suggestions on how to organize a system of SSTs, coordinate teams with schools, maintain communication with teams and team leaders, and support the success of the initiative. We also provide guidelines on creating a candidate pool of school support team members with sample nomination forms, communication and data collection instruments, activity logs, and sample school visitation agendas.

Chapter 3 presents detailed information on how to design professional development and training programs for school support team members. Drawing upon the experience of conducting more than 50 SST institutes, we present sample agendas for professional development for SSTs and other school change agents, detailed descriptions of field-tested activities, together with handout materials.

Chapter 4 provides additional clarification for your questions. And, last, the Appendixes contain sample training materials, transparency masters, organizational forms, and examples of instruments and procedures created by leading educators in the field. We invite you to adapt these to your own setting.

As you read the book, we encourage you not only to learn about new opportunities for Title I schools but, most important, to consider ways in which the SST model can support school improvement in any setting and in any community.

1 School Support Teams and Schoolwide Programs: A Window of Opportunity

Overview of School Support Teams

Too often federal legislation dictates what educators do, how they do it, and what happens if it is not done. Rarely does legislation provide structures that build our capacity to improve teaching and learning in schools. In this regard, Title I of the recently enacted Improving America's Schools Act (IASA) may prove exceptional. In addition to providing schools greater flexibility in the use of federal resources, this new legislation requires states to establish systems of intensive and sustained support for schools that receive Title I funds (see fig. 1.1). School support teams are to become the primary component of these systems (Public Law 103-382, Section 1117c 1994). Relevant sections of the law may be found in Appendix A.

The support teams are to assist schools as they plan, implement, and improve schoolwide programs—approaches in which high-poverty schools use Title I and other federal education resources to support comprehensive school reform. Schoolwide programs provide the opportunity to integrate school planning and improvement activities in ways that increase the capacity of an entire school to ensure the academic success of all students. This is in sharp contrast to traditional Title I/Chapter 1 approaches that provide auxiliary programs targeting services exclusively to students who meet district-defined eligibility criteria.

School support teams—external groups of teachers, pupil services personnel, and other persons with expertise in school reform—provide support and assistance to the staff of high-poverty schools as they plan and develop their schoolwide programs. Congress clearly wanted schools to be thoughtful about their many options for improving teaching and learning through schoolwide approaches. Thus, schools are required to plan over a one-year period and to engage external assistance in the planning process. SSTs are to increase the likelihood that new flexibility will be used in ways that lead to substantial increases in student achievement.

FIGURE 1.1—CHANGES IN CHAPTER 1/TITLE I

Before the Improving America's Schools Act (IASA), Chapter 1 was a program focused on

- Remediation
- Pull-out programs
- Centralized control
- Compliance and sanctions
- Restricted use of federal funds

Now, as Title I, it is a program based on

- A whole-school approach to improvement
- An engaging, academically challenging curriculum for all students
- The reduction of pull-out classes
- Site-based planning with parent and family involvement
- High-quality professional development
- Flexible use of supplementary state and federal funds
- Intensive support by teams of external facilitators

A Process That Can Benefit *All* Schools

The school support team concept and the school-wide change concept are not limited, in usefulness, to high-poverty schools. Although technical details such as funding options may vary from other whole-school restructuring processes, we believe that the principles and ideas in this book can be applied to any school change process. Educational researchers have consistently documented that when the total school is the target of school substantive change, schools can become positive learning environments for all students. Therefore, much of the information that this book offers about schoolwide programs is applicable to any school change process. Similarly, current literature on professional development stresses the importance of ongoing, sustained support for schools as they organize and initiate their own change efforts. Just as important, working with a school over a period of time can provide important insights into one's own practices and bring multiple benefits to a sending school, school district, or organization. SSTs are a viable profes-

sional development option for any school engaging in self-study or restructuring.

A Case Study

The following scenario exemplifies just one of several ways a school support team might work with a school.[1]

Hope Middle School

Anne Benally remembered a time when she felt differently. She recalled an interview for the principalship at Hope, her confidence and passion for making a difference in the lives of students. It was only four years ago, and now her greatest reward was a day without a crisis. And yet she had enough of a spark to agree, if reluctantly, to have a school support team work with her school as they initiated a comprehensive planning process for school improvement. She didn't know what to expect, nor did she expect much.

Ms. Benally was surprised when the phone call came from the SST coordinator. There was something different about the tone of the conversation. It wasn't dictatorial or bureaucratic, punitive or condescending. "Hello, Ms. Benally. This is José Villarreal. How is it going today? I'm glad you invited me to work with your school in your planning process this year. Your decision obviously reflects a level of trust, and I will honor that trust by being a true partner in helping you to bring about the kinds of changes you would like to see." Ms. Benally asked questions about the process, and Mr. Villarreal provided clear answers, often explaining that Ms. Benally and her school improvement team would own the decision-making process from the very beginning.

The first step was for Ms. Benally and her staff to select the other members of the school support team. Ms. Benally wanted another principal from a

---

[1]The names of the school and the people in this case study are pseudonyms.

high-poverty middle school, and team members selected Barbara Orozco from a list provided by the SST coordinator. For three consecutive years, the state had recognized Ms. Orozco's school because of her students' high level of academic achievement. Several of the teachers had heard wonderful things about the district's new parent liaison, Nick Johnson, so he was added to the list. Also, Mr. Villarreal recommended including Dr. Pat Sorenson from the local university because her expertise in math might help school staff understand and strengthen the low performance of Hope students on various math assessments.

Ms. Benally felt reasonably confident meeting with Mr. Villarreal for the first time. She and Mr. Villarreal had worked together to create an agenda for the first meeting. Throughout preliminary dialogue, Mr. Villarreal had clearly established that this process was not about evaluating, judging, or even recommending. The purpose was to support the staff and community of Hope Middle School in identifying and attaining their goals for academic improvement.

Even with all of the preparation, however, the first meeting of school support team members, staff, and parents was intense. The four team members were introduced to the entire staff at a faculty meeting. Three parents who participated on the school's improvement council were also at the meeting. Despite all of the preparation, there was an atmosphere of caution. This caution began to ease when school staff, parents, and school support team members introduced themselves and team members offered introductory comments that reflected a helpful attitude.

After the meeting, school support team members met with a small group of school representatives to learn more about the accomplishments of Hope Middle School. Staff and parents had prepared a school profile, similar to a portfolio, that contained the school's mission statement, agendas, and photographs of important events; samples of original work from teachers and students; and special

accomplishments of school staff and parents, such as the new community partnership program that pairs students with local establishments for job-embedded academic enrichment. The team felt inspired by the strong foundation upon which planning could be based.

Next, team members toured the school individually. With a guide, each team member became familiar with the building, met teachers and students in classrooms, visited the library, spoke informally with counseling staff about their goals and challenges, and talked to several teachers during their planning periods. They also talked to parents, the principal, and the school nurse. Throughout all of these conversations, the support team members listened as school personnel, parents, and students talked about their school, its strengths, its challenges, and its potential. Favorite questions were, "What is one thing that an outsider might not know about your school just by looking in?" and "What is one thing you are doing at Hope Middle School that you are most excited about?"

At the end of the day, everybody came together for a meeting. Mr. Villarreal and other support team members talked at length about many of the positive attributes of Hope Middle School. They had looked beyond the obvious challenges and identified strengths that were rarely acknowledged.

After they had spent half an hour discussing strengths, Mr. Villarreal shifted the conversation by saying, "Just as we know that Hope Middle School has many strengths, we also know that you are not satisfied with current levels of performance. Many of you shared with us today that you want more for your students. Let's talk about what you want for Hope Middle School, what you would like this school to be, and what you would like your students to achieve. What is your dream for this school?"

The next hour was filled with stirring comments from parents, teachers, counselors, paraprofessionals, and Ms. Benally. They wanted a school without violence, without fear—a school where learning was fun, and students, staff, and administrators enjoyed being. They wanted a school that the community would consistently acknowledge for its academic achievements and its civic contributions. They wanted a school of which they could feel proud.

After listening intently, Dr. Sorenson broke the team's silence by expressing her belief that the school could become all that it had articulated. She said that she had seen several other schools with fewer strengths accomplish similar goals. Mr. Villarreal added, "The goals you articulated are very attainable. We believe we can assist you in attaining those goals. We would like to support you if you are interested in building upon your successes and reaching for your goals."

Mr. Villarreal explained a planning process that had been helpful with other schools. He described a very comprehensive needs assessment process, a process for establishing specific goals, a strategy for expanding the school's understanding of options, and a process for reviewing progress. He explained that the staff and parents of Hope Middle School would need to assume responsibility for each step of the process but that the support team would be there to provide guidance and assistance. He reiterated that "whatever plans are developed will be your plans, not mine nor those of any members of the support team." The meeting ended with some dialogue about timelines, meeting dates, and next steps. There was a sense of excitement and anticipation, but Ms. Benally also knew that a lot of hard work was about to begin.

She was right. It wasn't an easy year. It would have been less complicated if the school had conducted a one-dimensional needs assessment, as it did every year for federal program compliance, but the support team had urged the school to look at more complex information. The school staff had been encouraged to discover the strengths that were buried in dismal looking statistics. They had been encouraged to weed out the needs that were hidden under glossed-over generalities about acceptable performance.

It would have been easier if the school had selected simple, easy-to-achieve goals, the kind that looked for small improvements on the fringes, while the major fabric of the school remained unchanged. The support team, however, consistently asked, "Would achieving that goal allow you to feel good about your work at Hope Middle School?" In addition, the team repeatedly reminded the school leaders of the many strengths that had been unearthed in the needs assessment process. Support team members asked, "If you could achieve this level of success in one class, why not in two—or in several?"

Once challenging goals were established, a period of anxiety began. Ms. Benally and several teachers and parents recognized that they would need to make real changes. For a while, almost everyone in the school felt like a researcher. Teachers were investigating approaches they had heard were successful in neighboring schools. Other teachers reviewed the literature on topics that seemed critical to the school's success. Parents met with Ms. Benally to brainstorm ideas for improving relationships between the school and families. The support team members kept providing new ideas and encouraging the extensive exploration of options. They stayed in touch with the school throughout the year, alternately acting as sounding boards, coaches, resource providers, and facilitators of planning and problem solving.

Toward the end of the first year, some difficult discussions about priorities and resources took place. Decisions were ultimately made that resulted in changes in job descriptions, changes in programs, and even changes in the daily schedule. Ms. Benally and members of the school's improvement council were pleased to see most of the changes. They had known for years that many of them needed to happen; however, they had not had the supporting data to withstand the political pressure that was surely to follow. Now they had a wealth of data, the support of numerous staff and parents who had been involved in the planning process, and an expanding network of educators to whom they could turn for ideas, resources, facilitation, and support.

When the year ended, Ms. Benally knew that she was ready to lead the school in new and dynamic ways. She believed once again that she could make a difference at Hope Middle School. In fact, she knew she already had.

Reflections on the Case Study

The case study illustrates the basic purpose for school support teams: to assist schools in catalyzing substantive schoolwide change that responds to a challenging vision of high student performance for *all* learners. All schools, no matter how demoralized or successful, have the potential for dramatic improvement. SSTs can help unleash this potential in a manner that leads to informed planning and inspired implementation. There are several reasons why this is so.

• Perhaps one of the most exciting aspects of school support teams is that *educators from different educational venues* work together to support change. Teachers, pupil services personnel, administrators, postsecondary instructors, and other people knowledcdgcablc about school change engage in interactive dialogue with school staff. The rich array of perspectives can far exceed the impact of a single outside change agent.

• *School support team members are not simply "outside experts."* They are educators, many of whom work in schools daily, with practical experiences and a range of resources on many topics. Although research on educational change is inconclusive about the ability of "outside experts" to influence school change, a school support team functions in a manner that sharply contrasts with the work of many topic-specific consultants who facilitate isolated, single-issue inservices.

• Ideally, *SST members affect the cultural and ethnic diversity of the schools they serve.* This effect can be especially important in communities where the teachers are largely European American but the students and community are made up of people of color. School support team members bring their experiences and expectations to the consciousness of the schools they serve.

• *Team members are essentially volunteers.* Their generosity seems to be primarily motivated by a genuine commitment to educational success for all students, by the opportunity to share their successes, and by the opportunity to learn from others. One of the most exciting consequences of school support teamwork is that the teams become a learning community as well as a teaching community.

• School support team members develop personal relationships within a school community. This means that, collectively, *they are able to understand the complex needs and issues of a school in a reasonably efficient manner.* (Imagine how many different voices can be heard when a team of five or six members is reaching out to the school community.) In many cases, school support teams are also able to interact with different levels within a school district (i.e., the school board, superintendent, principal, and teachers). These added perspectives further contribute to a multidimensional view of strengths, needs, and opportunities.

For a synthesis of information on the role of school support teams in Title I schoolwide planning, please see Moffett (1996).

Organizing a Statewide Program: The Texas SST Pilot Initiative

The Texas School Support Team Pilot Initiative is one of several SST initiatives in the United States. Although other models exist, Texas, with its 20 regional education service centers, provides a generous if not exhaustive perspective on different approaches to organizing, implementing, and reflecting upon the school support team process. These approaches do not require state-level initiation. As mentioned earlier, the SST process can benefit *any* school or school district as a new and vital form of staff development. We encourage schools and school districts, as well as state-level personnel to apply aspects of the Texas SST initiative to their own unique interests and needs.

Begun with a pilot during the 1994–95 school year, the Texas SST initiative has recently completed its first year of large-scale statewide implementation. The pilot included 12 high-poverty schools that were invited to receive assistance from school support teams. Pilot staff selected a pool of support team members from volunteers from education service centers, colleges and universities, and high-achieving Title I schools. Each support team was chaired by a facilitator from the Texas Education Agency (the State Department of Education in Texas). The facilitators participated in professional development on a variety of issues including school change processes, group facilitation skills, and relevant changes in Title I. This training was followed by a similar, but condensed two-day session for all members of the support team pool.

Each facilitator conducted a previsit to his or her assigned school. During these visits, the facilitators met with the principal and other school personnel to explain the purposes of the visit, plan the initial team visit, and select support team members that the school believed would provide the best customized support. Once the team was selected and dates were agreed upon, a full-team visit was conducted. Each initial two-day visit included an entrance meeting in which the support team met the school staff; campus tours; individual or small-group interviews with teachers, support personnel, parents, and administrators; and a planning meeting at the conclusion of the visit. The purpose of and approach to the visits varied slightly depending upon the needs of the school, as identified in previsit discussions. Consistently, however, the initial full-team visit was structured to assist the school in the initial phases of the planning processes and to strengthen the foundation for ongoing substantive decision making. After the visit, support team members provided phone support and helped school staff access materials and resources that might assist them in the planning process. The team conducted a follow-up visit to further assist the school personnel in their planning.

The first year of large-scale implementation included several different models, coordinated by the 20 regional education service centers in Texas. The goal was to create many different models that respected local needs while building upon the lessons learned through the pilot. Thus, SSTs were organized differently based upon the resources of each education service center, the number of schools needing assistance, and the preferences of local administrators. The length of visits ranged from a half day to two days at a time. Teams were led by service center staff, district-level personnel, or school-based educators.

Despite the diversity in organization and logistics, the approaches taken by the SSTs were strikingly similar. To facilitate coordination among the 20 education service centers, the Texas Education Agency hosted monthly two-way audio/two-way video teleconferences. These meetings provided SST organizers and trainers opportunities to learn from one another, articulate concerns, and share solutions. In addition, semi-annual meetings were held in conjunction with the Association for Compensatory Educators of Texas Conference to assist coordination. Throughout the year, the U.S. Department of Education's Region 8 Comprehensive Technical Assistance Center and its predecessor, Region E Chapter 1 Technical Assistance Center, assisted the education service centers as they conceptualized models, resolved logistical challenges, and provided professional development to more than 2,000 SST members. These supports provided the education service centers opportunities to build upon one another's strengths and learn from one another's experiences.

Issues Critical to the Success of SSTs

Questionnaires and focus groups from the Texas SST Pilot Initiative yielded valuable information from SST coordinators, school-based participants, and SST members that is influencing the development of systems of support in Texas and several other states. This information, when aggregated with recent data collected after the first year of large-scale statewide implementation, offers clues for success that may be valuable as other states develop their own initiatives, or as other systems of external change catalysts assist schools with systemic change (Ginsberg and Anderson 1995). The most recent data were collected through focus groups of SST coordinators from the 20 regional education service centers throughout Texas. Although regional models vary, and continue to evolve, preliminary analysis of data suggests that the following considerations are critical to the success of support teams in actualizing their potential to help improve teaching and learning in high-poverty schools.

Building Trust

Lasting change is most likely to occur in an atmosphere of openness and trust. If school personnel perceive a support team as a group of monitors or investigators, such trust is not likely to materialize, interactions are more likely to be perceived as aversive, and schools are more likely to maintain defensive postures. An atmosphere of trust and mutual respect must be established if schools receiving assistance are to openly share their concerns, fears, and dreams for the future.

School support teams throughout Texas are discovering that trust is most easily developed when everyone involved in the process clearly understands the purpose of the team, how a visit might be conducted, who might be involved, and why. Early, frequent, and clear communication is essential. In addition, there appears to be great value in developing, with a school, a clear and purposeful agenda that reflects a school's strengths as well as its challenges. The Texas initiative has found that a previsit from a support team coordinator provides not only the opportunity to meet with school staff and negotiate a mutually acceptable agenda for the full-team visit, but also helps to allay fears that the

SST process is somehow synonymous with state- or district-level monitoring visits.

Perhaps, most critical to establishing trust is for school support team members to convey an attitude of respect for the accomplishments, challenges, and autonomy of the schools they support. Professional development should assist team members in demonstrating a commitment to listening more than talking, observing more than reporting, and identifying strengths as well as respectfully identifying needs.

Facilitating Understanding of Strengths and Needs

In school improvement processes, educators frequently focus on identifying needs or weaknesses. Yet some of the most promising school improvement processes, such as Henry Levin's Accelerated Schools Model, emphasize the importance of building upon strengths (Levin 1991, Saxl et al. 1989). In the Texas SST initiative, emphasis is generally placed on building the capacity of schools to identify and understand their strengths, as well as their needs.

School staffs are encouraged to look at themselves from different perspectives. They develop portfolios or profiles to communicate their accomplishments, and sometimes they develop a personal case study to analyze for previously unrecognized strengths. They learn to take new looks at student achievement data and identify accomplishments, even in areas where accomplishments are not easily apparent. School personnel then conceptualize how they might build upon those strengths and promote their transfer and expansion to other classrooms within the school, other grade levels, other student groups, and other curriculum areas. This positive approach provides often-needed recognition for dedicated efforts, while encouraging growth in areas of need.

Facilitating Understanding of Potential for Excellence

The Texas SST initiative is designed with the belief that just as every child can learn and achieve at high levels, every school can become a place where all children achieve at high levels. In Texas we found that often educators had lost sight of their potential to make a powerful difference in the lives of children. School support teams can assist educators in rediscovering their potential for developing rich learning environments in which all children succeed.

One of the exciting attributes of school support teams is their capacity to dispel myths about limitations. Because the SSTs in Texas include educators from high-achieving Title I schools, the support teams were often uniquely qualified to assist school staff in broadening their perspectives about how much children can learn and how much schools can teach. School personnel have revealed their myths with statements like the following:

• "These children cannot be expected to achieve at such high levels because of their severe home situations."

• "We're doing about as well as can be expected with such a high-poverty school."

• "Given the language background of most of our students, we're not likely to ever reach the state's achievement goals."

• "Achievement at our school is always going to be limited because of high mobility and a lack of parental involvement."

School support team members from high-poverty rural and urban schools serve as living proof that such statements were wrong. There is strong evidence that in Texas, team members are being heard as they affirm that (1) yes, there are difficult barriers to be confronted, (2) similar barriers are being overcome at similar schools in which SST members work or have worked, and (3) there is good reason to believe that the particular school being assisted has the potential to overcome those barriers as well.

Encouraging Exploration of Options

It is easy to be convinced that the way we have always done things is the only way things can get done. Yet, we can also be reasonably certain that if we continue to use the same approaches, the same instructional practices, and the same organizational strategies, we are likely to attain the same levels of student achievement. Important challenges for school support teams, then, are to help school personnel explore promising new options for increasing student achievement and to make decisions that can lead to trustworthy evidence of success.

School support teams have a singular opportunity to help educators discover and examine alternatives for improving teaching and learning. In some cases, educators may be unaware of legitimate options for selecting innovative instructional materials, exploring instructional approaches that engage and challenge diverse learners, organizing time and space for substantive and/or community-based learning, structuring the use of fiscal resources for maximum impact, and effectively responding to conflicts among various stakeholders. School support teams can encourage the thoughtful consideration of alternatives by offering new ideas, providing literature and materials, and creating environments in which educators feel comfortable suggesting their ideas to colleagues. Perhaps the most important question team members can ask is, "Why not?" Too often, excellent ideas are rejected before they are aired because of inaccurate notions about what is or is not workable, legal, affordable, or otherwise practical. By asking "why not?" SSTs encourage schools to consider the potential of their imagination and creativity.

The Texas SST coordinators consistently agree that support teams must do more than give schools options to consider. The Texas experience confirms the need for SSTs to build the capacity of schools to identify and explore alternatives for themselves. One way that they can build such capacity is by assisting the school in becoming a learning community. By co-creating approaches to individual or collective inquiry and modeling collaborative decision making, teams can encourage a school to develop in-house sustainable approaches to professional development and to see itself as the locus of control for initiating change. A starting point for several teams has been to encourage schools to establish formal and informal structures that provide forums to explore diverse perspectives and ideas. By supporting schools in becoming more systematic inquirers into classroom practice and more skillful decision makers, SSTs can extend their impact far beyond the immediate needs of the schools served.

Enhancing Commitment

If SSTs do their jobs well, the schools receiving support will have a high level of commitment to a plan of action that substantively influences the academic success of all students. Texas SST members found that a school's personnel must perceive the school plan as their own. In every aspect of a plan of action, school personnel must recognize their own ideas, their perceptions of their needs, and their perceptions of their strengths. They must see the plan as both workable and important. Moreover, each staff person must see the importance of his or her contribution to the successful implementation of the plan. Without such commitment, the work of the SST will become another disconnected process, resulting in another plan to be filed away with all of the other plans completed to meet someone else's requirements.

The Texas experience provides evidence of the substantial potential of SSTs to provide meaningful assistance to high-poverty schools. Many of the schools that received assistance are actively pursuing the further development and implementation of promising schoolwide programs. At the same time, the Texas experience also reveals that the work of providing genuine support is difficult. It would be easier to establish "support" systems that were in essence monitoring systems; however, the experience of the past 30 years should help us know the limitations of such approaches. Educators in high-poverty schools need and deserve real support to improve teaching and learning. If high-poverty schools are to become places where virtually all

children achieve at the high levels expected in more affluent communities, school personnel must have

- strong support that allows them to build upon the strengths of their students and communities and to recognize their potential for academic excellence;
- access to a broad base of information about instructional, curricular, and organizational options; and
- high-quality support in the development of their own realistic plan of action for improving teaching and learning.

School support teams can provide such support.

School Support Teams in the Context of Federal Education Programs

SSTs have the potential to influence dramatic changes in the effectiveness of any school; however, recent changes in the Elementary and Secondary Education Act (ESEA) create an environment that increases the need for and potential benefit of such teams. Figure 1.2 illustrates these changes and the implications for school support teams.

Federal Education Programs Before 1995

Prior to the enactment of the recent amendments to the ESEA, schools were required to use most of their federal education resources in separate categorical programs. Federal laws and regulations required that only those students who met strict eligibility criteria could benefit from these programs. Thus, to ensure compliance, students were often pulled out of regular classrooms to receive special services. Sometimes students participated in so many special pull-out programs that their regular classroom teachers believed they did not have any real opportunity to be accountable for the achievement of these students.

Teachers were also frustrated because students who met the mandated eligibility criteria were often not the ones with the greatest need for the particular

Elementary and Secondary Education Act Prior to Improving America's Schools Act Amendments	Elementary and Secondary Education Act Since Improving America's Schools Act Amendments	Implications for School Support Teams
Few schools could be schoolwide projects.	Any Title I school where more than 50 percent of the students live in poverty can become a schoolwide program.	Schools must engage in an extensive planning process with the support of a school support team or other technical assistance provider in order to become a schoolwide program.
Programs were categorical and separate. There was sometimes duplication of services from multiple programs.	In schoolwide programs, there is much greater opportunity to combine and coordinate federal program funds to improve teaching and learning at the school.	Support teams must help schools with schoolwide programs reconceptualize how Title I and other federal programs can work together to support state and local school reform efforts.
Eligibility criteria limited access to services from various programs. Students needed the right label in order to use equipment, work with personnel, or otherwise benefit.	Schools with schoolwide programs have the opportunity to determine which services will best benefit which students. Students do not need any label in order to receive any benefit.	Support teams must help schools with schoolwide programs reconceptualize ways to ensure that every child gets access to the services needed to ensure high levels of academic achievement.
Services were primarily provided through pull-out programs. These programs focused heavily on low-level skills.	In schoolwide programs, schools may choose from many organizational, curricular, and instructional strategies that lead to the attainment of challenging academic skills. Emphasis is placed on professional development designed to increase the capacity of personnel to work effectively in new systems.	Support teams must help schools carefully examine options so that decisions are made that will result in all students attaining challenging academic skills. Support teams must promote sustained, intensive, high-quality technical assistance that improves the capacity of personnel to work effectively in new systems.
Federal programs were often planned and managed from the district's central office to ensure compliance with federal requirements.	Each school with a schoolwide program is given substantial flexibility for defining its own programs and the use of its resources. Parents, teachers, and students must be involved in planning efforts.	Support teams must ensure high-quality involvement from all groups in the planning process. Support teams must facilitate the development of strong partnerships among all stakeholders.
Accountability was focused primarily on compliance issues.	Accountability is focused primarily on student achievement.	Support teams must assist the school in establishing ongoing mechanisms for gauging student progress and adapting accordingly.

service. Thus, computer labs were sometimes empty because the lab was purchased with federal fund X and only students labeled X could use it, or instructional aides were idle because the aide was hired with federal fund Y and only students labeled Y could receive his or her assistance. Auditors sometimes made split-funded personnel feel as if they should be plugged into a logging device that allowed them to properly account for every minute spent.

In many cases, pull-out programs were characterized by a focus on remedial instruction. The pace of instruction was reduced, the level of academic challenge was lessened, and expectations for achievement were adjusted to create situations in which students would be more likely to "feel successful." In reality, many students got further behind academically with each year of their participation in the special programs. Program evaluations focused on measures of achievement that were frequently alien to the curriculums and goals of regular classrooms. Thus, even when evaluation results showed minimal gains, these gains frequently did not transfer to regular classroom performance.

To ensure compliance with the complex and confusing federal regulations, school districts hired central office administrators who were given the mandate of making sure that teachers and principals resisted their impulses to find creative ways to use the federal funds, except for the narrow uses that seemed "safe" from potential audit exceptions or compliance violations.

Federal Education Programs Since 1995

On July 1, 1995, most of the provisions of the Improving America's Schools Act of 1994 became law. These amendments resulted in the most dramatic changes in the 30-year history of the ESEA. The amendments gave schools the opportunity to reconceptualize the use of many of their federal resources in ways that focus on improving the capacity of the entire school to improve the academic achievement of students.

Most of the changes were focused on schools in which a large percentage of students lived in poverty. These schools were given substantial flexibility through provisions in the law that allowed for schoolwide programs. Previously, schools in which 75 percent or more of the students lived in poverty could become schoolwide projects. Under the amended law, schools in which 50 percent or more of the students live in poverty can become schoolwide programs. In many school districts, most or all of the district's Title I schools can become schoolwide programs.

Schoolwide programs have the challenge of determining how their federal resources can be used to support overall reform efforts in ways that are consistent with the intents and purposes of the federal legislation. No longer are schools required to perceive the federal programs as separate programs, with distinct goals and special evaluation criteria. Instead, schools can think of their federal programs as a set of coordinated tools for pursuing locally defined school improvement goals in concert with state and district accountability systems. Although each federal program must be accounted separately (as before), schools have much greater opportunity to combine and coordinate programs in ways that complement school reform efforts.

Through schoolwide programs, schools can move beyond burdensome eligibility criteria and accompanying labels to approaches that improve teaching and learning in every classroom to ensure that every student attains challenging academic goals. Focus is not on watered-down curriculums or low-level skills; rather, it is centered on challenging curriculums and accelerated instructional approaches that help students close the achievement gap with their peers in more affluent communities.

Overwhelmingly, the new ESEA emphasizes accountability for increased student achievement in contrast to accountability simply for compliance. The new law gives principals, teachers, and parents much greater opportunity and responsibility for using their federal resources in ways that build upon the unique strengths and adapt to the unique needs of their students. Site-based planning with the substantial involvement of families is required.

The Need for School Support Teams in Schoolwide Programs

Schools do not automatically become schoolwide programs and acquire the associated flexibility. Each school that wishes to become a schoolwide program must engage in extensive planning. The law mandates that the planning process involve the individuals who will be implementing the plan (teachers, administrators, counselors, and other support personnel) and the individuals who will be served by the plan (parents, secondary school students, and community members). Further, the law specifies that schools receive assistance through the planning process. This assistance is most likely to be provided through school support teams.

Although teams can benefit any school, the potential benefit is most impressive in schools that are planning or refining schoolwide programs. At each schoolwide program, SSTs may influence change in the use of thousands of dollars of federal and state resources. Teams are responsible for helping schools engage in a meaningful planning process. The result of that process is a well-integrated plan of action for increasing the likelihood that every student will attain challenging academic standards. School support teams have the opportunity to

- Involve schools in concentrated efforts to study their own strengths and needs,
- Challenge schools to establish exciting goals,
- Guide schools through detailed inquiry processes that carefully examine new options,
- Assist schools through complex decision-making processes that take advantage of accumulated knowledge,
- Support schools through the implementation of new approaches, and

- Lead schools through processes that allow them to reflect upon and refine their efforts to improve schools.

SSTs have an extremely important role in helping make the new ESEA work. These teams will provide the guidance, support, and encouragement that will help schools step beyond tradition and comfort and pursue research-proven approaches for improving teaching and learning throughout the school. Further, recognizing that change is not easy, SSTs will provide the ongoing support that helps schools learn from their practice so that academic growth is continuous and powerful.

One of the important roles of the support team is to assist the school in developing a comprehensive schoolwide program plan for reforming the total instructional program in the school. The plan must list all of the federal, state, and local programs that will be included in the schoolwide program; include a comprehensive needs assessment of the entire school with data related to state student achievement standards; and describe

- How the school will use Title I and other resources to implement the schoolwide program plan;
- Schoolwide reform strategies that will be used to help all children attain state achievement standards;
- Instructional strategies to increase the quantity and quality of learning time, provide enriched and accelerated curriculums, and address the needs of all students, particularly those from historically underserved populations and populations targeted by federal education programs;
- Strategies that will be used to meet other student needs (e.g., counseling, mentor services);
- Strategies to determine if student needs have been met;
- Strategies to be used to ensure that staff providing services are highly qualified;
- Strategies for improving the involvement of families in the education of their children, including

the parental involvement policy to be developed jointly with parents;

- Plans for assisting preschool children in the transition from early childhood programs to kindergarten (for elementary schools);
- Strategies for including teachers in decisions regarding the use of additional assessments (beyond those required in the state Title I plan);
- How the school will provide individual assessment results and interpretations to parents;
- Strategies for providing timely additional assistance to children who experience difficulty during the school year; and
- How the school will disaggregate assessment results by gender, major ethnic/racial groups, socioeconomic status, language background status, migratory status, and disability status, and report statistically sound data to the public.

Once the plan is developed, the school support team periodically works with the school to review progress and recommend improvements. The plan is neither written by nor implemented by the team. The plan must belong to the school. Instead, the support team has the important role of providing high-quality support throughout the plan's development and implementation. Appendix B provides useful overheads for assisting schools, school districts, school support team members, and state personnel in understanding the features of effective schoolwide programs, recommended steps in planning, and some of the challenges.

The Need for School Support Teams in Other Title I Schools

Each state's system of school support teams is to provide assistance primarily to schools planning or implementing schoolwide programs. If funds are available, however, teams may also assist other schools in which a high percentage of students meet poverty criteria or schools in need of improvement.

Most high-poverty Title I schools are likely to choose to become schoolwide programs; however, some may choose to remain targeted assistance schools. If more than 75 percent of the students attending a targeted assistance school meet poverty criteria, the school can receive assistance from a school support team (if the state determines that funds are available).

The law also specifies that school support teams may provide assistance to schools in the school improvement process. Each state is required to establish a system for determining if schools are making adequate yearly progress toward getting all students to attain the state's academic standards. Schools that fail to meet this standard for two consecutive years enter into a school improvement process. Schools in the school improvement process (and other schools in need of improvement) may also receive services from school support teams. In these cases, the team is responsible for helping the school develop and implement a plan for improving academic achievement at the school.

2 Making It Happen

Overview

At first, it may appear overwhelming to organize a system of school support teams, coordinate teams with schools, maintain communication with teams, and learn about how to best support the supporters. Our experience has taught us that an SST initiative takes on a life of its own shortly after the process begins. Although it is useful to have trusted and creative colleagues with whom to share ideas, much of the process is self-sustaining once you put it into motion. In part, this result may be attributed to the fact that team members tend to be reasonably sensitive, confident, and collaborative educators. This is one of the reasons that they, themselves, have experienced success. They need structural/procedural support and an opportunity to learn from one another's experiences, but SST members generally have a knack for understanding educational strengths and challenges. And, typically, they are respectful of how vulnerable school-based educators are to criticism. Most schools *and school support teams* are nervous as they approach the first visit but feel the affirmation of their worth and potential upon its conclusion. An SST coordinator needs to be accessible to encourage, organize, and problem solve, but does not need to micro-manage.

Getting Started

There is no one way for getting started. The following considerations provide a compass rather than a map to guide SST coordinators. We are cautious about being overly prescriptive because the beauty of this initiative is its responsiveness to the unique conditions of planners, SST members, and schools. This is a process that must be customized to respond to the unique opportunities and challenges within each state, region, or school district. Our experience has taught us that key steps for beginning to organize a school support team initiative include:

- Identify a process for recruiting members,
- Create a nomination form for potential applicants,

• Identify a leader for each team,

• Develop ways to organize and coordinate the work of multiple teams,

• Provide initial professional development for team members,

• Develop communication tools for use within each school to be served as well as between SST members and the SST coordinator,

• Develop a procedure for handling fiscal issues related to time and expenses of members,

• Initiate contact with schools eligible for SST assistance,

• Anticipate challenges, and

• Provide follow-up support for members after they have begun their work.

Identify a Process for Recruiting SST Members

School support team membership is generally a voluntary process. There are several approaches to identifying and recruiting members.

• If a candidate pool is being developed across an entire state or region, letters can be sent to central office administrators, administrators at distinguished schools, deans of education at colleges and universities, executive directors of regional education service centers or cooperatives, executive directors of regional educational laboratories or technical assistance centers, representatives of professional organizations, and outside consulting groups.

• When the initiative is hosted by a school district, rather than at the state or regional level, it is advantageous to invite superintendents and other key district personnel to an introductory meeting. This is a chance not only to introduce the SST opportunity, but also to listen to their concerns and work together to overcome challenges, such as ways to release teachers from their classrooms on a regular basis.

• Within school districts, superintendents or SST district-level contacts frequently suggest using site-based decision making teams as SST members. One Texas district pairs schools so that each school

has the benefit of working with the other's site-based team.

Ideally, however, teams are composed of educators from diverse venues. Therefore, it may be desirable to add other experienced educators to a site-based team if it is to become a school support team. And, of course, there is much to be said for word of mouth. Our best thinking on recruiting members suggests that you use multiple approaches. Whichever approaches are used should reflect understanding of two critical issues:

1. Administrators will allow their talented teachers, counselors, principals, professors, or consultants to pursue SST responsibilities *only* when the administrator sees value for his or her administrator's organization. Thus, superintendents, deans, service center directors, and other key administrators must be helped to understand the value of participation to their organization's goals.

2. Talented educators will volunteer to participate on SSTs *only* when they see the support team as a powerful opportunity to share what they have learned with colleagues and to learn more as they work with other educators. Thus, emphasis must be placed on the potential value of their participation not only to the schools they serve, but also to themselves and their educational institutions. Working with another school as an SST member can be a professional development experience in its own right. Team members grow professionally as they facilitate creative decision making with school improvement teams. The learning goes both ways. (Please refer to Appendix C for a sample State-Level Letter of Introduction and Appendix D for a sample Regional- or District-Level Letter of Introduction.)

Create a Nomination Form

A nomination process is helpful in communicating that high caliber individuals are being sought for SSTs. Also, a nomination process helps ensure a well-balanced pool of SST members, reflecting diversity in demographics, experience, and expertise. We have found that although it can be useful to have educators with specific skills on school support teams, most educators have a range of expertise that they have developed from experience. While nomination forms allow SST coordinators to know for certain that they have a range of members with varied specialties, members are not intended to be "experts." The goal is for the school to see *itself* as the expert, that is, to become skillful at posing critical questions and locating resources. This outcome is important logistically, because time constraints frequently prevent SST coordinators from being able to construct the exact kind of team a school might initially identify for support. A sample Nomination Form for School Support Team Members is provided in Figure 2.1. Another sample nomination form is provided in Appendix E. Appendix F offers a sample Response Form for Participation on a School Support Team for use by interested team candidates.

Identify an SST Leader for Each Team

The leader for each team plays a pivotal role in serving as a liaison with the school and with the SST coordinator. We recommend that the team leader initiate a personal meeting with school leadership prior to the full-team visit. This can be collaboratively facilitated with a district-, regional-, or state-level SST coordinator. We also recommend that the leader initiate a dialogue with SST members to assist them in defining their own unique roles and responsibilities. As the liaison between the team and the SST coordinator, typically the leader is the person who synthesizes information and regularly communicates with the coordinator. The following list may be useful as a reminder to SST leaders who wish to develop a packet of pre-visit information for team members:

- Letter of introduction from the coordinator
- Entry visit agenda
- Campus profile information
- Planning form
- SST Member's Log.

Develop Ways to Organize and Coordinate the Work of Multiple Teams

This topic can require a sense of humor if teams are being coordinated at a state or regional level and there are large numbers of schoolwide programs to serve. If this is the case, a state or regional agency may need to initially prioritize who will be served. Appendix G provides a typical map for creating a manageable SST system. Appendix H offers a sample tool that the system coordinator can use to communicate with teams as they become increasingly autonomous. Appendix I provides a sample letter to assist coordinators in communicating with team members once they have been selected for an initial visit. We know of several districts that are working in a reciprocal relationship to send teams to one another's schools. The possibilities are limited only by the boundaries of our imaginations. Suggestions for creating a manageable plan for coordinating SST services follow. They may be particularly useful for creating a regional initiative.

1. **Develop and disseminate a survey** to schools and local education agencies (LEAs) that provides information on SSTs and simultaneously addresses the schools' (a) awareness of the schoolwide option, (b) awareness of the schoolwide planning process, (c) current involvement in schoolwide planning, (d) interest in schoolwide planning, (e) interest in SST support for schoolwide planning, (f) willingness to involve key school and district personnel, as well as parent and community leaders, and (g) willingness to allocate time for teacher involvement in planning and related professional development.

2. **Create a multi-layered approach** that responds to schools according to individual needs and priorities. Schools may wish to have preliminary planning to support the development of a comprehensive needs assessment, yet others may request immediate and sustained support. In this way, regional service agencies could phase in comprehensive, sustained support over time with possible demonstration sites once the process gets under way.

FIGURE 2.1—NOMINATION FORM FOR SCHOOL SUPPORT TEAM MEMBERS

Name: _____ Social security number: _____

Address (work): _____ Phone (work): _____

_____ Fax: _____

Position: _____ Campus: _____

District: _____ City: _____

Please indicate the number of years of work experience in each area:

____ Elementary school   ____ University

____ Middle school   ____ Education Service Center

____ High school   ____ Other: _____

Please check your areas of expertise:

Content Areas	Programs	Strategies
❑ Reading/language arts	❑ Title I (Chapter 1)	❑ Cooperative learning
❑ Mathematics	❑ Gifted/talented	❑ Site-based planning
❑ Science	❑ Bilingual	❑ Conflict resolution
❑ Social studies	❑ Migrant	❑ Classroom management
❑ Other: _____	❑ Special education	❑ Campus improvement planning
	❑ Inclusion	❑ Parental involvement
	❑ Resource	❑ Technology
	❑ Schoolwide	❑ Authentic assessment
	❑ Other: _____	❑ Other: _____

3. **Determine a priority system based on level of commitment** as well as on poverty level and eligibility as a schoolwide program. Criteria for demonstrating commitment might be based on (a) a commitment to a three-year relationship with the SST, (b) administrative commitment to encouraging and supporting risk-taking, (c) development of and support for a site-based committee, and (d) allocation of resources for teacher release time and professional development.

4. **Develop a first-year transition system** with a manageable number of SSTs with the goals of piloting a purposeful, clearly conceptualized approach; creating mentor sites for eventual school-to-school support; and preparing current members to become leaders the following year so that, for example, 10 SSTs of 5 members each can become 50 teams the following year, with prior support team members serving as team leaders.

Provide Initial Professional Development for Team Members

This topic is described extensively in Chapter 3. Time permitting, we recommend that initial training include philosophical and legislative foundations; a clear statement of purpose; opportunities for the SST to imagine visiting a school and to practice facilitation skills; an exercise that examines what works with school reform and promotes insight into the change process; approaches to substantive school improvement planning; and opportunities for prospective SST members to define and articulate the personal and professional significance of the SST initiative.

Develop Communication Tools for Use with Schools and Teams

There are several kinds of communication needs. One need is for SST members to have a working document that allows members of a team to plan for their school visitation experience. Figure 2.2 is a sample School Support Team/Campus Leadership Team Planning Form. SSTs may want to have some

data in advance of visiting a school. A Campus Profile Information Form, similar to the one provided in Appendix J, has been useful to several teams. This form provides insight into demographic and quantitative data that offer a more complete picture of the school context. It also provides space for SST members to gain a sense of a school's (1) access to community resources, (2) professional development experiences, (3) campus initiatives, (4) special programs on campus, and (5) parent/family/community involvement program. The form also helps team members identify what a campus believes about its strengths and priorities for improvement based on its mission statement.

A third communication need is twofold. SST members will want to note interactions, insights, and requests they receive from the schools with which they work. SST coordinators will want a way to review the overall process in order to continuously improve upon it and knowledgeably respond to phone calls and other inquiries. The sample School Support Team/Campus Leadership Team Planning Form in Figure 2.2 can also assist with goal setting and between-visit follow-through. It was intentionally created to be a very general document in order to maximize flexibility. The sample School Support Team Member's Log shown in Figure 2.3 is a useful tool for helping team members easily summarize interactions, including phone calls, fax exchanges, meetings, site visits, or resource distributions.

And, finally, SST coordinators may want a form that can assist their record keeping of team composition, the focus of visits, and their progress in assisting schools with the steps of schoolwide planning. The Program Description Guide provides a place to start, and a sample can be found in Appendix K.

Develop a Procedure to Compensate SST Members for Their Time and Expenses

The SST process is essentially volunteer in nature. It is a powerful professional development opportunity for SST members and members of a receiving

FIGURE 2.2—SCHOOL SUPPORT TEAM/CAMPUS LEADERSHIP TEAM PLANNING FORM

Goals	Next steps	Who will oversee it?	How will we know if we're successful?	Timeline

Figure 2.3—School Support Team Member's Log

SST member _____

Address _____

Phone # _____

Campus contacted _____

Person contacted _____

Date _____

❏ Phone call/FAX   ❏ meeting   ❏ site visit   ❏ resource distribution

❏ other _____
(specify)

Length of time _____

Number of people _____

TOPICS _____

_____

_____

Summary of interaction _____

_____

_____

_____

_____

_____

_____

_____

_____

_____

_____

_____

_____

After this contact is made, please return this form to:

_____

_____

_____

school. Even so, there may be state-, regional-district-, or school-level funds to reimburse team members for travel and release time, especially for school personnel. In many states, Title I funds are used at state, regional, and local levels to support the process. State directors of Title I and regional or local federal program personnel can provide the necessary clarification for this option. An approach many districts or receiving schools select is to reimburse team members for substitute time and for travel that exceeds a certain mileage radius.

Initiate Contact with Schools Eligible for SST Assistance

This process requires a simple letter, fax, e-mail message, or announcement to introduce the opportunity, and then a follow-up phone call or visit to speak with a school principal. It is particularly useful to enclose a stamped, addressed post-card for recipients of letters to return to the SST coordinator. Postcards can provide a simple check-list that indicates preferred visitation dates or the preferred focus of an initial team visit. Most initial announcements are highly personable and provide a concise overview of the purpose of an SST, its composition, and services/resources it can provide. A note of caution: Many schools, especially those that are experiencing inordinate challenges, construct clear boundaries between themselves and anyone who might be perceived as a critic. Until trust is established, even the most enlightened SST process may be, at best, cautiously received.

We strongly recommend that the school support team leader arrange a personal meeting with the principal to share information about the SST opportunity and to listen to the principal's questions and suggestions about the ways in which a team might support the school's goals. We also recommend collaboratively sketching an agenda with the principal and other school representatives for the initial visit. Having an agenda helps to make the possibilities for interaction concrete and com-

fortable for the school community by following the school's lead. Figure 2.4 presents a sample Entry Visit/School Support Teams Agenda for a first full-day visit. Once a tentative agenda is conceptualized, we recommend a preliminary discussion of the kinds of expertise a school would most appreciate. If it feels right, participants may want to agree upon a possible timeline for site visits. This is also a good time to encourage a principal and school represen-tatives to work together to consider how they might engage others in the school community in dialogue about changes that can make a real difference and ways to free people up so that they have adequate time to plan and to learn together. The most fre-quent question we are asked is how to develop trust between the SST and individuals in the school. We believe that there is something to the old adage, "People don't care how much you know until they know how much you care." Once your foot is in the door, school support teams have to earn the privi-lege of serving as coaches and facilitators. We believe that it is a good sign when school people want to be certain that they are the decision makers and they control their work.

Anticipate Challenges

Anticipating challenges is active learning at its best. Where people accept challenge and take risks, even those risks that hold great promise, it is necessary to develop safety nets. We encourage SST coordinators to establish up front

- Opportunities for team members to learn with and from others;
- Regular planning meetings with colleagues;
- Ways to ensure worthwhile, participatory meetings;
- How participatory decisions will be made;
- How SSTs and school improvement teams can locate resources and develop a resource file;
- How to plan professional development and support for "the supporters" (e.g., SST members);
- How to chart the initiative's progress in ways that sustain momentum;

FIGURE 2.4—ENTRY VISIT/SCHOOL SUPPORT TEAMS AGENDA

- Welcome/Introductions

- Icebreaker

- Review Agenda

- Purpose/Goals

- Campus Portrait

- Campus Expectations of School Support Teams

- Review Campus Plan/Vision

- Campus Priorities for Improvement

- Discussion/Details of the Day

- SST Members Tour Campus and Visit Staff, Parents, and Community Members

EXIT MEETING—Toward the End of the Day

Topics:

- Welcome Back!

- Purpose

- Sharing Experiences

- Discussion of Strengths

- Discussion of Priorities for Improvement

- What Next?

- Plan Second Visit

- Closure

- Approaches that everyone can agree to for solving problems;
- Productive procedures for dealing with complaints;
- Approaches to dealing with conflict.

Provide Follow-Up Support for the Supporters

Participants in an SST initiative actively work with others to construct models of change, shape new ideas, and internalize possibilities. This is exciting and ambiguous work that requires ample communication with others who are similarly engaged. Members and coordinators need to share ideas and experiences with others if an initiative is to grow. We believe that the Texas School Support Team Pilot Initiative, now in its third year, has evolved from teams of apprehensive participants to communities of active learners because of opportunities to work together to create a shared knowledge base and learning context. The 1996–97 learning context for the regional coordinators of school support teams in Texas, for example, is made up of quarterly two-day work sessions. Work sessions provide the organizers of regional initiatives an opportunity to collaborate on a series of questions they wish to examine. The questions represent the range of experiences with school change processes and SST implementation. Each roundtable dialogue group of SST members and coordinators prioritizes questions according to its own interests and immediate needs. Typically, however, no question appears too big or too small to be of benefit to everyone.

Possible Topics for Dialogue

Recent questions from an SST coordinator work session consisting of roundtable dialogue groups follows.

About the Logistics of Coordinating SSTs

- What are some of the ways that Education Service Centers can organize SSTs to efficiently and effectively serve many schools?

- What are some different ways to construct teams?
- How are agendas created and communicated so that an SST and a campus will have a sense of how to proceed once the team arrives?
- What does—or might—a sample visitation agenda look like?
- Is there a tool or a guide that assists team members in helping campuses to identify strengths and needs?
- Have you developed a record-keeping system for your SST process, and if so, what does it involve?
- Have you developed a process for communicating with team members?
- Have you had to deal with conflict as you coordinate SSTs, and if so, have you learned something that may be valuable to others?
- What resources on teams or on teaming have been useful to you?
- What resources on school change have been useful to you?

On Working with Schools That Are New to Schoolwide Planning

- When you work with individual schools that are new to schoolwide change, how do you generally begin?
- Do you have a specific approach to help schools identify and prioritize areas for schoolwide (or school improvement) planning?
- What are some of the ways that you develop trust and rapport with schools?
- How do you—or might you—assist schools in building commitment to substantive planning?
- How are schools in your region learning about opportunities related to schoolwide change?
- How are you trying to communicate with large numbers of schoolwide programs or schools that are planning schoolwide programs?
- How are some of the schools in your region that are most actively engaged in the change process learning about ways to help all children reach high standards of academic success?

Making It Happen

Experience has shown that one of the best ways to support school support team initiatives and keep the momentum going is to provide frequent opportunities for coordinators to communicate with one another about the ways they are approaching their work with support teams and schools. These interchanges have happened in face-to-face facilitated meetings, as well as by phone, fax, e-mail, and video-teleconferencing. Experience has also shown that support teams like to hear about the experiences of other teams, as well as maintaining regular communication with one another.

This chapter has provided several examples of approaches to communication used by SST coordinators. The possibilities for creating supportive and constructive communication opportunities, however, are endless. This chapter has also delineated the organizational issues related to school support team planning and implementation. If nothing else, the issues we have featured illustrate that this is a process that stimulates imagination, invention, and trust in our collective capacity to make it happen.

3 Designing Professional Development for School Support Teams

Emerging knowledge about the nature and purposes of learning has caused us to think carefully about the kind of professional development needed to prepare school support team members to work with schools. If we wish to encourage educators to move toward active, constructivist, performance-based, integrated, and collaborative methods of learning, then we must *model* these more effective approaches to teaching and learning in preparing SSTs.

Underlying Beliefs Guiding School Support Team Preparation

A guiding question for designing SST professional development is, "What are the approaches to teaching and learning that we hope to inspire?" We suggest approaches that are philosophically aligned (e.g., intrinsic motivation, integrated curriculum, and constructivist learning) so that they naturally work together to create a community of learners engaged in active inquiry. This is most likely to occur when prospective members participate in professional

development experiences that allow them to feel respected and connected to one another, see new ideas as relevant and challenging, and experience their own personal and professional effectiveness. This approach is based upon the basic principles of human motivation to learn, both across and within cultures (Wlodkowski and Ginsberg 1995).

Thus, this chapter presents ideas, agendas, and resources for preparing members that incorporate experiential, participatory learning activities, such as case studies, cooperative and collaborative learning, structured opportunities for participants to share expertise, and time for reflection and constructing personal meaning about the ideas offered to them. Our goal, whether instructing SST members or working directly with schools, is to model, support, and encourage the best that we know about teaching and learning.

In addition to considering the question of *how* best to design SST professional development, we also need to selectively consider *what* knowledge and skills will help team members be most effective as facilitators of school growth and change. This is a challenging task, given the breadth and depth of the existing knowledge base and resources on such topics as facilitation skills, team building, problem solving, decision making, school improvement planning, the change process, staff development, systems thinking, and promising new initiatives in teaching and learning. Compounding the challenge of designing focused and relevant training is the fact of limited time. Most SST members—busy professionals in their own right—have restricted schedules and a range of responsibilities in their own schools or organizations. Thus, we have found through experience that they prefer a one-day orientation to their voluntary role as members of school support teams, rather than more extended time away from their primary commitments.

This chapter focuses on what we have learned to be most useful in developing an initial knowledge and skill base in educators new to the school support team process. In it you will find sample workshop agendas, the topics that prospective members and coordinators have found most useful, a variety of field-tested professional development activities successfully used in professional development programs, and a range of options for designing one-day, two-day, and follow-up training sessions that are tailored to the needs of your own setting.

Useful Topics for Professional Development

The following concepts and topics are common to the more than 50 introductory sessions that new school support team members have participated in over the past three years:

• **Creating a clear sense of purpose based on legislative and state-specific policy.** It is critical for people to know why they are doing what they are doing. Like a compass, a clear sense of purpose allows us to end up where we intend without restricting inventiveness by being overly prescrip-

tive. When we understand the purpose for doing something, we can be more confident, creative, and effective in aligning our actions and goals. Clarity of purpose for school support teams is also valuable because it reduces confusion with other teaming initiatives.

• **Distinguishing the school support team process from the processes of monitoring and evaluation.** Some teaming efforts in public education are oriented toward monitoring school effectiveness or compliance with the use of state or federal funds. Several states, for example, have accountability teams for these purposes. Although some of the most innovative state accountability initiatives are forging collaborative relationships with schools as they evaluate school effectiveness or the use of state or federal funds, it is important to distinguish the school support team process from evaluative processes. The purpose of SSTs is to help schools to question themselves—not to monitor or enforce compliance. The goal is to support—not judge—schools so that they may make their own decisions about how to help all students achieve academic success.

• **Understanding the potential of teams to influence school change.** Although the idea of collaboration is not new, many educators have not had an opportunity to consider how teaming can contribute to the effective decision-making processes of others. Professional development exercises that allow SST members to explore the potential of a team approach to assisting change undergird a team's ability to believe in, articulate, and work toward exemplary team practices.

• **Understanding SSTs in relation to other models or networks of professional teams.** Building an awareness of other models or networks of professional teams—for example, the League of Professional Schools (Carl Glickman) and the Coalition of Essential Schools (Ted Sizer)—can strengthen the

SST members' distinct sense of purpose and, at the same time, build connectedness to the national movement toward teamwork to foster professional development (see Lasoff, Olson, and Sommerfield 1994; Lieberman and Grolnick 1997).

• **Reviewing information about Title I opportunities that extend beyond a "fix-the-child" orientation to positively influencing teaching and learning throughout an entire school.** Many members of SSTs are new to Title I. For many, Title I still signifies the trailer on the playground to which designated children periodically rotate. SSTs need to be aware of how the new law supports whole school reform if they are to help schools comprehensively plan for schoolwide change. When bold, new ideas are introduced, SST members need to feel empowered to say, "Why not?"

• **Understanding the change process—what works and what doesn't work in school reform.** The ultimate goal of SSTs is to serve as catalysts for meaningful school reform. Team members need to understand the complexity of change and apply research-based lessons to their own experience. They need to understand that what works in one setting may not necessarily apply in another; that change is rarely, if ever, a linear process; that conflict and resistance are predictable and inevitable when attempting a school improvement process; that problems are also an inevitable part of change and, therefore, need to be reframed as opportunities for creative thinking; that organizations don't change until the individuals within them change; and that a repertoire of strategies is needed for dealing with the complexity of helping a school move from where it is to where it wants to be.

• **Developing a collective philosophy for working effectively with schools.** A strength of SSTs is the diversity of experiences, perspectives, and talents on a simple team. At the same time, members must have a unifying philosophy that guides

how they approach working among themselves and with schools. Having such a philosophy helps team members and school sites feel the kind of purpose, direction, and interpersonal ease that can lead to genuine collaboration.

• **Developing approaches to establishing trustful relationships between school support teams and schools.** Lasting change is most likely to occur in an atmosphere of openness and trust. If schools perceive the school support team as a group of "monitors" or "investigators," trust will be impaired because school members will assume defensive postures. Developing a sense of reduced threat and openness—essential for working together—will help school members share their concerns, fears, and dreams and encourage them to take challenging risks.

• **Developing approaches to assist schools in devising or further considering challenging visions of high student performance.** This is the essence of the role school support team members can play. A school community must have shared passion for learning about new ways to approach teaching and learning and for taking action to improve student performance. This involves more than locating materials, information, and equipment. It involves modeling high expectations for both adults and children and facilitating stimulating opportunities for examining bold new ideas.

• **Developing thoughtful questions to help schools consider options and rigorously test their assumptions, ideas, and hypotheses.** The way in which questions are phrased can support or impair consideration of strengths, needs, and options. When questions are phrased to reinforce successes and to initiate dialogue about how school members understand certain challenges, there is a likelihood that schools will participate in the inquiry process as an opportunity rather than a threat. Additionally, SSTs have the opportunity to help schools conceptualize strategies for identifying and testing their unproven assumptions. SSTs help schools get beyond the TTWWADIs (that's the way we've always done it) and identify more powerful options for improving student achievement.

• **Developing approaches to enhance schools' commitments to and capacity to oversee their own change processes—so that over time the role of the school support team diminishes.** One of the primary purposes of SSTs is to assist schools in empowering themselves as the locus of control for innovative and equitable decision making. Teams must safeguard against usurping the authority of others. They must help schools to develop their own participatory processes of inquiry and decision making and to recognize the connection between their decisions and short-term and long-range school improvement, so that schools will be better able to trust their thinking. Ultimately, the need for external support should diminish as the skills and vision of those within the school grows.

• **Respecting the school as the locus of control for decision making.** Schools must see themselves as the locus of control for change, if innovation is to become a part of the school culture. This is one of the reasons why SST members need to act as facilitators of change rather than as providers of solutions to challenges that other people face. If members of the school community do not view a plan for school improvement as uniquely their own, commitment to implementation will be marginal at best.

• **Identifying success.** Motivation theory teaches us that adults, as well as children, must be able to identify the fruits of their labor. Although some of our most worthy decisions have abstract consequences, we must look for concrete evidence of effectiveness based on indicators established in advance, and help schools to do the same, in order to support and validate the hard work of change. Helping schools identify small successes, as well as larger ones, also provides the needed impetus for moving forward in the improvement process.

• **Customizing the features and logistics of a district's, region's, or state's SST model.** School support team members need to learn from the experience of SSTs in other states and districts, as well as from their own experience, as they negotiate the complex logistics of providing meaningful support across districts, regions, or states. At the same time, teams need to be encouraged to customize their processes to meet the needs of the school with which they are working so that these processes are viewed as practical, relevant, and worthy of enduring.

Professional Development Activities for Preparing SST Members

Given the scope of knowledge and skills needed, designing learning opportunities for school support teams is clearly a challenge. Experience has taught us that it is best to *do less* and do it well than to provide superficial coverage of a great deal of information during training sessions. The sample Agendas for School Support Teams Institutes provided in Figure 3.1 (pages 42–43) are drawn from three years of experience in designing professional development activities for school support teams. Both agendas—a one-day and a two-day professional development institute—assume that the training is for new members wishing to refresh their memories and expand their repertoires of approaches for working with schools.

The agendas include a variety of activities to help school support team members

• Understand the concepts of schoolwide planning and school support teams;

• Work collaboratively with schools in a manner that is supportive rather than judgmental;

• Plan bold, new schoolwide programs that address the needs of all students in the school while simultaneously improving the academic achievement of targeted student populations previously served under Chapter 1 categorical funding programs.

School support team instructors will need to select those topics and related exercises that are most appropriate for their own unique purposes, participants, and time constraints. The topics outlined on pages 28–30 of this chapter are all of potential worth to prospective team members. Trainers will need to select those that are most important, given the prior knowledge, experience, skill level, interests, and time constraints of their group.

What follows are detailed descriptions of the purposes and processes of a range of activities so that you can customize your SST staff development program based on your own priorities and scheduling constraints.

Activity 1: Venn Diagram Sharing

Purpose: To create a sense of community among SST members; to set the tone for engaging in open, supportive communication; to provide members with multidimensional sharing processes for building rapport with and among school community members at visitation sites

Time: 30 minutes

Format: Triads with large-group debrief

Materials: Newsprint, markers, paper, and pens

Process: Venn diagram (fig. 3.2, p. 44).

The facilitator asks the entire group to consider the concept of culture and factors that might influence their cultural identities. People will normally suggest such possibilities as gender, socioeconomic class, ethnicity, language, music, religion, food, and home of origin. We emphasize that culture is a complex concept and cannot simply be reduced to a list of nouns or adjectives, but that for the purpose of this exercise, a list helps people select topics that they can easily explore together.

The facilitator writes down approximately 7 to 10 words that people call out. Then the large group

divides into groups of three, and each group draws a Venn diagram. Each triad member selects one of the three circles to represent himself or herself. All three then select topics from the list of words that the large group has generated and begin to identify ways in which they are similar and unique from one another. Unique qualities, such as languages spoken or ethnicity are entered on the portion of a person's circle that does not overlap anyone else's. Qualities that are shared by two group members—for example, gender for persons one and two, are entered in the space intersected by the two people who share a common quality. When all three group members have something in common, they locate it in the in the center of the diagram where the space is intersected by all three circles. Participants are encouraged to share information only on those topics that are comfortable for the whole group.

After 15 to 20 minutes, each person reflects for a short time on something that he or she learned from participating in the exercise. Some generalizations occur more frequently than others: "We realized that we had more in common than we might have predicted," or, with respect to SSTs, "We need to find ways to help people in schools know more about one another. The more information people have about one another, the more they are likely to give one another a break." There is no limit to what might be said. Many people like the idea of using a Venn diagram to focus the dialogue because it reduces self-consciousness, provides a safe structure for self-disclosure, and encourages participation (Ginsberg and Wlodkowski 1995).

Alternate Introductory Activity: Think, Pair, Share

Purpose: To provide participants with an opportunity to develop rapport with one another while at the same time considering questions that are relevant to school change or that they could use in their own school support team visitations

Time: 15–20 minutes
Format: Pairs with large-group debrief
Materials: Overhead or flip chart, markers, paper, and pens
Process: Reflection and sharing.

Select *one* of the following questions. Ask SST members to briefly write a response on paper, share the response with a nearby person, and collectively summarize shared and new ideas.

During the large-group debrief, record responses on a flip chart or an overhead. Recommended questions include:

1. What are some of the material possessions or opportunities that you now enjoy that would not have been as likely to occur in your life in the year that you were born?

Debriefing Question: What are one or two thoughts that occur to you as a consequence of reflecting on this question? What can we learn about change from this exercise? What are the implications of this exercise for schools?

2. What is one particularly interesting thing about your school or community that an outsider would not realize at first sight?

Debriefing Question: What are the implications of this exercise for schools that receive SSTs? What are the implications of this exercise for SST members?

3. Think of a time when you felt wise, creative, humorous, and able. Describe the experience.

Debriefing Question: These are attributes associated with the natural desire to learn. What conditions helped to create these at-

tributes? What does this mean with respect to creating classrooms where all students feel motivated to learn?

4. Visualize the elementary or high school that you attended as a child. Visualize the elementary or high school in which you now work. What are the similarities and differences?

Debriefing Question: What do participants' responses suggest about school change? How might SSTs use this question during a school support team visitation?

Activity 2: Creating a Clear Sense of Purpose Based on Legislative and State-Specific Policy

Purpose: To explore the origin and purposes of school support teams as conceptualized broadly by the federal government in the Title I reauthorization, and more specifically by each state; to create a collective orientation to providing support that is consistent with legislative and local intent
Time: 15 minutes
Format: Brief lecture, individual "quick-write," large-group debrief
Materials: Overheads of Section 1117 of the IASA; quick-write paper and pens (a quick-write is a one- to two-minute written reflection on an issue or question); flip chart and markers
Process: On an overhead projector, briefly review the key points of Section 1117 of the Improving America's Schools Act (IASA). (See Appendix L for Overheads of Section 1117 of the IASA. Note: The complete text of IASA Section 1117 is in Appendix A.) Ask SST members to do a two-minute quick-write of why they

believe these teams are considered necessary for school reform. Ask members to share their responses with a person nearby when they are ready. Invite volunteers to share their responses with the whole group. Record the responses on a flip chart.

Alternate Activity: Reviewing Brief Statement of Purpose for School Support Teams

Format: Individual review of information and large-group debrief

Materials: 3x5 cards, flip chart, markers

Time: 15–20 minutes

Process: Ask SST members to read through the sample Statement of Purpose (fig. 3.3, p. 44) *twice*—once to get a general sense of the vision, and a second time to focus on detail. In a large group, ask members to paraphrase key points or words for the group to remember. Record ideas on an overhead or on newsprint. (Sample responses include "commitment," "empowerment," "school-based decision making," "school ownership.")

Next, ask the group to individually consider and note, on 3x5 cards, ways to protect the purpose or vision. Collect the idea cards in a basket, and ask for volunteers to draw three or four suggestions to read aloud as a sample of the group's thinking. Ask the volunteers to post the cards with tape on the wall of the meeting room for the group to review at break time. Sample responses include:

• "Ask SST members to maintain a unity of purpose by restating their understanding of the purpose of SSTs prior to school visits."

• "SSTs need to be flexible in helping schools consider options and remember to ask members of the school community 'Why not?' if they think they cannot try something that they would really like to try."

• "SSTs need to work together to make their interactions with schools purposeful. Clearly specified roles and tasks for members can help with this."

If time and group size permit, SST members may want to work together to identify themes that they recognize as they review the cards.

This is a good time to distinguish SSTs from other teaming processes that may already exist in your state. For example, many states have state-level or state-sponsored teams for compliance and monitoring purposes. Many districts use vertical team processes for encouraging, for example, math teachers of grades 9–12 to align their curriculums. Nationally, the teaming process most similar to the SST model is the Critical Friend process (Senge 1990, Costa and Kallick 1993). A Critical Friend is a trusted person whom a school invites to ask provocative questions, provide data to be examined through another lens, and offer a critique of a person's or school's work, as might a friend. The extent to which SSTs act as critical friends varies among states, regions, and districts. Regardless, several states stress that the goal of support teams is to help schools to understand their strengths and to identify, for themselves, areas of need. It is more facilitative than evaluative.

Each school receiving assistance from an SST has the opportunity to use its Title I resources in new and creative ways that could lead to powerful differences in student achievement. The schools receiving assistance are all eligible to become schoolwide programs, if they are not already ones. They all have a substantial need to increase student achievement. They all have unique challenges, and they have overwhelming potential for dramatic improvement. SSTs will help unleash this potential in a manner that leads to informed planning and inspired implementation.

Ultimately, the involvement of a school support team should lead a school to its own discovery and thorough understanding of its strengths and needs; its own delineation of a challenging vision of high student performance; and its own thoughtful consideration of options and commitment to actions that will bridge the gap between current performance and the challenging vision for all students. To facilitate such a difference, given the scheduling constraints of most educators, is an impressive challenge. This is why we are assembling a most impressive group of educators for each school team.

Activity 3: Creating a Context for Working Together to Help a School Identify Strengths and Needs

Purpose: To examine, through experience-based learning, how a team might work together to help a school identify strengths and needs

Materials: Case Study Scenario, Analysis, and Debrief

Process: Distribute the Case Study for the Montrose Elementary School Support Team (fig. 3.4, p. 45) and the Case Study Analysis Matrix (fig. 3.5, p. 46), and explain that the purpose of this exercise is to provide a context for team members to vicariously begin to work with a school as a team. The goal is for SST members to help a school deepen its awareness of ways in which it might build on its strengths to address its needs.

Help SST members form teams of five, and ask teams to select a facilitator, notetaker, reporter, and group process observer whose role it is to ensure the equitable participation of all group members. (Team members are encouraged to actively participate but always reserve the right to contribute in whatever way is most comfortable—including listening.)

Ask members to individually read the scenario twice—once for a general overview and a second time for detail. Using the analysis matrix, ask members to individually note, throughout the second reading, the *strengths*, *resources*, and *needs* of Montrose Elementary (a pseudonym). When members of a team have finished reading and taking preliminary notes, the facilitator leads the team in sharing its findings. They then work together to create questions that can assist a school, in a respectful and nonthreatening manner, in probing its strengths and further addressing its needs. After a reasonable length of time (approximately 25 minutes from the beginning of the exercise), team reporters share their group's findings for large-group consideration.

Debriefing the Case Study Analysis

For the large-group debrief, request two volunteer scribes to alternate the recording process in order to efficiently list each team's finding on newsprint.

Beginning with the topic "strengths," ask the reporters from each team to share two to three of the strengths it has identified. (Limiting responses gives members of each team an opportunity to contribute. At the end, the large-group facilitator can ask teams to contribute any additional ideas they might have.) Move next to the topic of "resources," and then to "needs," proceeding, once again, from team to team. Finally, ask teams to report the "questions" that they began to frame.

There are at least two ways to work with the topic of "questions." We mention to the large group that wording questions in the most supportive way possible is an evolving art. One of the benefits of questioning ourselves as we pose questions to others is that we become more adept at using language in ways we most value. As we share each team's questions, we can

1. Simply write down the questions as stated,

2. Write down the questions as stated but examine them later to further understand how they might be received and how they might be more effectively worded, or

3. Reword or reconceptualize questions as the group sees fit on an continuing basis.

Activity 4: Understanding the Potential of School Support Teams to Influence School Change

Purpose: To help team members clarify, through reflection and imagination, why the SST process is of benefit to themselves and others

Time: 45 minutes

Format: Small group

Materials: Overhead transparencies of the quotes in Step 1 or relevant quotes from any of the articles that follow; newsprint; markers; and tape for posting graffiti responses

Bibliographical Sources for Suggested Quotes:

Allen, L., and B. Lunsford. (1995). *How to Form Networks for School Renewal.* Alexandria, Va.: Association for Supervision and Curriculum Development.

Goodman, J. (1994). "External Change Agents and Grassroots School Reform: Reflections from the Field." *Journal of Curriculum and Supervision* 9: 113–135.

McLaughlin, M. (1990). "The Rand Change Agent Study Revisited." *Educational Researcher* 19: 11–16.

Moffett, C. (Winter 1996). "School Support Teams: Facilitating Success in High Poverty Schools." *ASCD Human Resource Development Program Professional Development Newsletter*: 1–2, 8.

Olson, L. (May 4, 1994). "Critical Friends." *Education Week*: 29–33.

Saxl, E. R., with M. B. Miles and A. Lieberman. (1989). *Assisting Change in Education.* New York: Center for Policy Research; Seattle: University of Washington; Alexandria, Va.: Association for Supervision and Curriculum Development.

Snyder, J. S., M. Giella, and J. H. Fitzgerald. (1994). "The Changing Role of Central Office Supervisors in District Restructuring." *Journal of Staff Development* 15: 30–34.

Process:

Step 1: To set the stage, select a transparency quote for SST members to briefly consider. Pose the

question, "Does this quote corroborate your own experience as an educator? Sample quotes, taken from the references listed, include:

"It is impossible to overestimate the amount of training, development, and support that schools teams need as they embark on collaborative change efforts. . . . It has become very clear that the key role in serious change is that of the facilitator—the person(s) from outside . . . the school whose job it is to provide . . . support and assistance in the long term and complex process of change."

—Saxl with Miles and Lieberman (1989)

"If you want to bring about fairly simple changes which are intuitive for people, then you can do it fairly briskly. But if the nature of the daily interactions between students and teachers, between students and technology, between teachers and teachers is going to be fundamentally different, people don't have experience in doing that. And if there is going to be more responsibility for placing education in the hands of local folks, then a McDonald's cookie-cutter kind of approach isn't going to work."

—Howard Gardner, Director of the Project Zero Group

"One of the things that invariably runs down innovation over time is a feeling of isolation. The people within a school have got to feel that there's somebody elsewhere that cares a lot about what they're doing and speaks their language."

—Robert E. Slavin, Success for All Network

Step 2: Mention that there are several informative references for "external change agents." Most, however, do not explicitly reference the role of external *teams* in school change. Nonetheless, you may want to remind SST members of the option to form, independent of the workshop, collegial groups for reading activities on facilitating change as an external change agent. Cites are included under "Materials."

Step 3: "Carousel Graffiti" Activity: Select approximately five questions from the following list that you believe to be most relevant to prospective members of school support teams. For example:

• How might the team process benefit schools?

• What might team members gain?

• How can members foster genuine collegiality between themselves and the schools they visit?

• What might schools want to know about themselves to inform the process of creating and implementing schoolwide innovations?

• What are some approaches to facilitate planning? (Help schools arrange "focused visits" to other schools, e.g., to observe some of the innovations they might like to try.)

• What challenges might members of a school site experience as they engage in active planning?

• How can an SST know if it is serving a school well?

(Although all of the questions listed above are worthy of consideration, we believe that *less is more*. It is easy to overwhelm the process by being too ambitious about what SST members need to know immediately. Our approach has been to select questions of the greatest personal relevance, to engender a clear sense of purpose, respect for the SST concept, and to help team members understand the richness of their own experience as it relates to their evolving SST roles. Experience with the several SST initiatives has taught us that because of the diverse composition of teams, members will be able to learn by doing—with the support of more experienced colleagues.)

Step 4: Using bright markers, write each of the questions you have selected for group dialogue across separate pieces of newsprint. Each piece of newsprint should contain only one question (i.e., five questions, five pieces of newsprint).

Step 5: Ask members of the large group to count off so that they can form five small groups. (The number

of groups must correspond to the number of questions selected.) When groups have been formed, give each group a piece of newsprint with a question on it.

Step 6: Tell all of the groups that in just a minute they will be asked to collectively address their questions. The process is called "graffiti" because they can record their responses to their question in any way they choose, including using symbols or other artistic representations—to the extent that others can understand their thinking. After each group has had approximately five minutes to discuss and respond to its question, the members will be asked to pass their question clockwise. Each group then considers its new question, adding to the graffiti of the previous group. After five minutes, they again will be asked to pass their question clockwise. This process continues until each group has had an opportunity to respond to all of the questions.

Step 7: Finally, each group will end up with its original question. The task, then, will be to briefly summarize all of the contributions. Because everyone will have already had an opportunity to think about each of the questions, the summaries ought to be concise statements or artistic representations that express identifiable themes or that draw a conclusion. Each group will need a reporter to share his or her group's summary, limiting the report to approximately two minutes. If space permits, graffiti re-

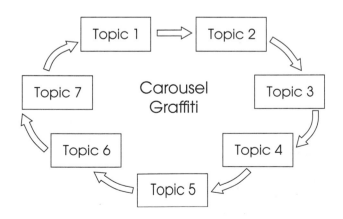

sponses can be posted around the room. Later, the information can be transcribed for further study.

Activity 5: Understanding the Change Process: What Works and What Doesn't in School Reform

Purpose: To review, through cooperative learning, a synthesis of research on school reform; to apply research on school reform to the SST members' roles as facilitators of schoolwide reform

Time: 45 minutes

Format: Cooperative learning

Materials: Discussion questions in Figures 3.6–3.7 (p. 47) and debriefing questions in Figures 3.8 and 3.9 (pp. 48–49). The article by M. G. Fullan and M. B. Miles, (June 1992), "Getting Reform Right: What Works and What Doesn't." *Phi Delta Kappan* 73: 745–752. (See Appendix M for a reprint of this article.)

Process: Distribute *Kappan* article to all participants.

Step 1: Ask participants to count off by fours. Each small group with members representing numbers 1–4 is the participant's original or "home" group.

Step 2a: In order to divide up the task, participants whose number is either 1 or 3 will read and discuss the section of the Fullan and Miles article on "Why Reform Fails."

Step 2b: Participants whose number is either 2 or 4 will read and discuss the introduction to the article and the section on "Propositions for Success."

Step 3a: Participants representing the numbers 1 and 3 form two separate subgroups and discuss the questions in Figure 3.6.

Step 3b: Participants representing the numbers 2 and 4 form two separate subgroups and discuss the questions in Figure 3.7.

Step 4: Participants return to their original home groups and share their discussions and insights regarding school reform and their role as program improvement facilitators.

Step 5: Participants share insights and strategies with the whole group (figs. 3.8 and 3.9).

Note: This cooperative learning exercise was contributed by Nancy Kraft of RMC Research Corporation, Larimer Square, Denver, Colorado.

Activity 6: Learning from Experience How to Develop Customized Approaches

Purpose: To provide members with a big picture of what an SST process might look like so that they can begin to construct customized approaches to working with schools

Time: 60 minutes

Format: Small groups construct graphic representations

Materials: Chart paper, assorted colored markers, and tape for each group. Copies of the Agenda for a School Support Team Visit (fig. 3.10, p. 50) and Recommendations from the Texas School Support Team Pilot Initiative (Appendix N)

Process: Collaborative "story boards" to create pictorial/graphic representations of approaches to working with schools

Step 1: As a precursor to this activity, ask SST members—in four separate groups—to review the outline of recommendations that were identified in the Texas School Support Team Pilot Initiative (Appendix N).

• Group 1 reviews "Creating Entree" (getting your foot in the door).

• Group 2 reviews "Building Relationships."

• Group 3 reviews "Facilitating Meaningful Planning."

• Group 4 reviews "Enhancing Commitment."

Ask SST members to note recommendations that they believe to be nonnegotiable, as well as any additional recommendations that can enhance the process. Ask volunteer scribes to transcribe as each group shares its nonnegotiables and additional recommendations.

Step 2: Arrange SST members in groups of four or five. Ask each of the groups to imagine that they are going on their first visit to a fictitious school—for which they will develop an original name. Explain to participants the context in which their visit will occur. For example, ask participants to assume that a previsit has been conducted by the SST coordinator in order to (1) explain the purpose of SSTs, (2) review campus data, (3) clarify campus priorities in terms of goals that it is working toward, (4) collaboratively plan an agenda for the first full-team SST visit, and (5) discuss ideas for a "campus portrait" that the school's improvement team can share with SST members. Figure 3.10 provides a sample Agenda for a School Support Team Visit. Ask members of each group to read the agenda, and imagine what their day might look like from the time they leave their homes until the time they return.

Step 3: Using newsprint and colorful markers, ask each team to draw—in any way they would like—their shared understanding of how a school visitation day might occur. Encourage creativity and humor, as well as the inclusion of any details that a team might want to include. For example, the SST might imagine a team breakfast meeting at a local restaurant prior to the visit, or it might imagine an interview process with one or two questions that could reveal perceptions of ways in which the school has been changing, and the relationship of past change efforts to student performance. This is an opportunity for participants to create their conception of an ideal day as school support team members.

Step 4: Ask each group to post its story board and

"appoint a volunteer" to tell the group's story, limiting themselves to five minutes. (We recommend that you designate a timekeeper who will notify each group when it has one minute left to conclude.)

Activity 7: Moving Beyond the "Fix-the-Child" Approach

Purpose: This section provides selected approaches that SST members can use to help schools rethink options and opportunities for improving teaching and learning throughout the school. It does not provide a detailed overview of Title I. This is provided in the first chapter, in Figure 1.2, and in the resource materials in Appendix A. We encourage team members to select information from the first chapter to use with schools as a general overview about the reasons for and the ways in which Chapter 1 has evolved into Title I. School staff must have foundational information. Overheads we have used to present an initial overview of the positive intent of the legislation are provided in Appendix L.

Time: 20 minutes

Format: Brief lecture

Materials: Overheads of Section 1117 of the Improving America's Schools Act (IASA) (Appendix L)

Activity 8: Personalizing the Potential of Schoolwide Programs

Purpose: To provide SST members with an initial activity to facilitate at the schools they visit in order to establish a positive orientation toward schoolwide change

Time: 45 minutes

Format: Carousel Graffiti

Materials: Graffiti questions written in advance on large sheets of chart paper; assorted colored markers

Graffiti questions:

1. What are two or three things that your school is doing to influence the quality of teaching and learning for all students?

2. What new ideas—based on something you have read, studied, or observed—have the potential to improve teaching and learning throughout your entire school?

3. What challenges might schools face as they plan for schoolwide change, and how might they overcome those challenges?

4. What resources are necessary for creating meaningful change that has the potential to improve teaching and learning throughout your entire school?

Step 1: Using bright markers, write each of the questions you have selected for group dialogue across separate pieces of newsprint. Each piece of newsprint should contain only one question (i.e., four questions, four separate pieces of newsprint). Ask the large group to count off so that they can form four small groups. (The number of groups must correspond to the number of questions selected.) When groups have been formed, give each group a piece of newsprint with a question on it.

Step 2: Inform the groups that in just a minute they will be asked to collectively address their questions. They can record their responses in any way they choose, using symbols or other artistic representations, as long as their thinking is clear to others. After approximately five minutes to discuss and respond to their question, each group will pass its question clockwise. Each group will then consider its new question, adding to the graffiti of the previous group.

Step 3: After five minutes, ask groups again to pass their question clockwise. This process continues un-

til each group has had an opportunity to respond to all of the questions. At the end of the activity, each group should receive the chart paper with its original question. The group's task, then, will be to briefly summarize all of the contributions. Because everyone will have already had an opportunity to think about each of the questions, the summaries ought to be concise statements or artistic representations that express identifiable themes or that draw a conclusion.

Step 4: Each group will need a reporter to share his or her group's summary, limiting the report to approximately two minutes. If space permits, graffiti responses can be posted around the room. The information can also be transcribed for future study.

Activity 9: Examining Key Components of Schoolwide Planning

Purpose: To cooperatively examine options and opportunities for two major categories of schoolwide planning and implementation: comprehensive needs assessments and general principals of school reform; to identify priorities for further study

Time: One hour, including a five-minute report by each group

Format: Study groups with Dialogue Guides and topical information

Materials: The two Study Group Dialogue Guides and related support materials in Appendixes O and P

Process: Divide groups into two areas of interest: comprehensive needs assessment and school reform. Ask each group to chose a facilitator, notetaker, and reporter and to collectively review (and modify, if desired) the instructions on their dialogue guide, prior to following written instructions. Directions for the school reform activity appear on p. 104. Please see p. 122 for the needs assessment activity.

Activity 10: Debriefing the Study Groups to Plan Next Steps

Purpose: To transform the recommendations of study groups into next steps

Process: Using Figure 3.11 (p. 51), a K-W-L strategy, as a planning instrument, ask the large group to identify what it knows, what it would like to know, and how it will proceed.

Materials: Individual planning sheets, overhead transparency of a K-W-L planning instrument, transparency markers

Time: 15 minutes

Activity 11: Creating a Restructuring Agreement

Purpose: To affirm commitment to schoolwide reform based on Title I and other restructuring principles

Time: 20 minutes

Format: Groups of two or three

Materials: Sample Restructuring Agreement

Process: Present the information in Figure 3.12 (p. 52) (Creating a Restructuring Agreement) for consideration, revision, and adoption prior to addressing restructuring goals.

Activity 12: Creating Time for Collaboration

Purpose: To encourage school staff to develop strategies for collaborative planning, teaching, and reflection for comprehensive and ongoing restructuring

Time: 30 minutes

Format: Groups of three

Materials: One copy per participant of the information in Figure 3.13 (p. 53), Strategies for Expanding Time for Collaborative

Planning, Teaching, and Reflection. Handout with questions 1–5 below.

Process: Ask school staff, in groups of three, to respond to the following questions and to add any additional questions they would like to consider:

1. What norms or traditional ways of organizing time make it challenging for adults in your school to learn and plan together?

2. How do you currently access the expertise and resources of personnel, family, or community members?

3. How might more flexibility with scheduling help members of your school community plan and work together in complementary ways?

Present Figure 3.13 handout to help school staff consider additional ways to allocate time to manage school improvement. Ask school staff, working in groups of three, to discuss:

4. What is one idea you would like to try in support of greater collaboration?

5. What would you need to do to make your idea a reality?

Transcribe group responses on newsprint. Ask the groups if they would like to initiate a process to further pursue some of the ideas about which they have expressed interest. If so, ask the principal and members of the school improvement team what they believe are the next steps for prioritizing goals related to time and initiating a plan. (Who needs to be involved who is not currently present? How might this best occur? Who will oversee the process? Who will assist? What tasks need to be performed in support of extended time for collaboration? How will communication occur so that all members of the planning process and school community remain informed?)

Activity 13: Action Planning

Purpose: To create a planning process that represents the perspectives of multiple constituencies

Time: 30 minutes

Format: Small groups

Materials: Action Plan: Planning to Plan template presented in Figure 3.14 (p. 54)

Process: Using Figure 3.14, facilitate a small- or large-group discussion to build consensus around each question.

Activity 14: Reflection and Closure Exercises

Purpose: To clarify and affirm individual learning; to affirm collective learning and the value of being a community of learners; to identify gaps in information; to shape future directions

Time: 15 minutes for individual writing; 5–15 minutes for large-group sharing

Format: Individual reflection and writing, followed by discussion

Process: Using the prompts in Figure 3.15 (p. 55), Reflection Log, ask participants to respond to items 1–6.

Alternative Activity: Head, Heart, Hand

Purpose: To encourage participants to reflect on personal applications and make a commitment to action

Time: 5 minutes for personal reflection; 10 minutes for large-group sharing

Materials: Prompts in Figure 3.16 (p. 56)

Process: Ask participants to use the prompts in Figure 3.16, Head, Heart, and Hand Activity, as a guide for reflecting on an activity (or the entire school support team training institute).

Resources for Schoolwide Improvement

In this chapter, we have presented the beliefs that guide our approach to professional development for school support teams—and we have outlined the content and skills that our experience has shown to be most useful in preparing individuals to serve as effective facilitators of schoolwide change. Finally, we have provided detailed descriptions of a range of participatory activities based on a constructivist view of learning, a respect for the existing professional and personal expertise of new school support team members, and a concern for providing teams with timely and relevant information to guide them in their work with schools.

All of the activities described in this chapter have been used successfully in professional development sessions we have conducted in a variety of settings. We encourage you to take the resources we offer here and tailor them to the needs of your own setting—whether that setting be preparing school support teams to meet the guidelines set forth in Section 1117c of the Improving America's School Act for high-poverty schools, or preparing external change agents to facilitate a thoughtful, collaborative, creative, and data-based approach to continuous growth and improvement in any school.

FIGURE 3.1—AGENDAS FOR SCHOOL SUPPORT TEAMS INSTITUTES

Sample Agenda for a One-Day Institute

9:00–9:15	WELCOME, GOALS, OVERVIEW
9:15–9:45	GETTING ACQUAINTED **Venn Diagram Activity**
9:45–10:15	SSTs: OPPORTUNITIES AND CHALLENGES **Brief Lecture and Small-Group Discussion** Overview of the concept of schoolwide programs and SSTs statement of purpose/vision for SSTs, followed by participants' restatements of the purpose/vision for SSTs in personal terms.
10:15–10:30	BREAK
10:30–11:15	CASE STUDY SCENARIO, ANALYSIS, AND DEBRIEF
11:15–11:50	VISITATION SIMULATION: Visual representation of a sample visitation.
11:50–12:00	REVIEW OF THE MORNING
12:00–1:15	LUNCH
1:15–1:45	CAROUSEL GRAFFITI Sample Questions: • How might the SST process benefit schools? • What might support team members gain? • How can SSTs foster genuine collegiality between themselves and the schools they visit? • How can an SST know if it is serving a school well?
1:45–2:30	WHAT WORKS AND WHAT DOESN'T WITH SCHOOL REFORM **Cooperative Learning Jigsaw with *Phi Delta Kappan* article by Michael G. Fullan and Matthew B. Miles, "Getting Reform Right: What Works and Doesn't Work"**
2:30–2:45	QUESTIONS & ANSWERS, FUTURE DIRECTIONS
2:45–3:00	CLOSURE

Sample Agenda for a Two-Day Institute

8:30–8:45	INTRODUCTIONS AND OVERVIEW
8:45–9:15	GETTING ACQUAINTED • **Venn Diagram Activity** • **Think, Pair, Share Activity** What is one unique thing about your school or school community that an outsider would not know in advance?
9:15–9:30	OVERVIEW OF SCHOOL SUPPORT TEAMS • Legislation • Philosophy • Opportunities

FIGURE 3.1—CONTINUED

9:30–9:45	OVERVIEW OF SCHOOLWIDE PROGRAMS
	• Legislation
	• Philosophy
	• Components of all plans

9:45–10:15   EXAMINING THE POTENTIAL OF SCHOOLWIDE PROGRAMS

Graffiti Questions:
1. What are 2 or 3 things that your school is doing to influence the quality of teaching and learning for all students?
2. What new ideas—based on something you have read, studied, or observed—seem exciting to you?
3. What challenges might schools face as they plan for schoolwide change, and how might they overcome those challenges?
4. What resources are necessary for creating meaningful change in schools?
5. What questions would you like to be sure to have answered by the end of the day?

Summary Question:
What are the implications of the graffiti (on your original page) with respect to schoolwide change?

10:15–10:30   BREAK

10:30–11:00   VIDEOTAPE: *COMMON MIRACLES*
Viewers of this tape learn how communities are addressing education reform using Howard Gardner's theory of multiple intelligences and other key school reform strategies.[1]

11:00–11:15   VIDEOTAPE DEBRIEF

11:15–11:45   CHANGE METAPHORS

11:45–1:00   LUNCH

1:00–1:45   MAJOR COMPONENTS OF A SCHOOLWIDE PLAN: STUDY GROUPS
• Comprehensive Needs Assessment
• Change
• Family Involvement
• Professional Development

1:45–2:00   REPORTING BACK FROM STUDY GROUPS

2:00–2:15   BREAK

2:15–2:45   PLANNING TO PLAN
• Phases of planning
• Creating a restructuring agreement
• Action planning

2:45–3:00   FUTURE DIRECTIONS AND CLOSURE

---

[1]For more information about *Common Miracles*, contact IRI/Skylight Publishing, Inc., 200 E. Wood St., Suite 274, Palatine, IL 60067. A useful video for developing effective classroom-based teaching and learning strategies for all students is *Encouraging Motivation Among All Students* (1995). For more information about this video, contact the Video Journal of Education at 1-800-572-1153.

FIGURE 3.2—VENN DIAGRAM

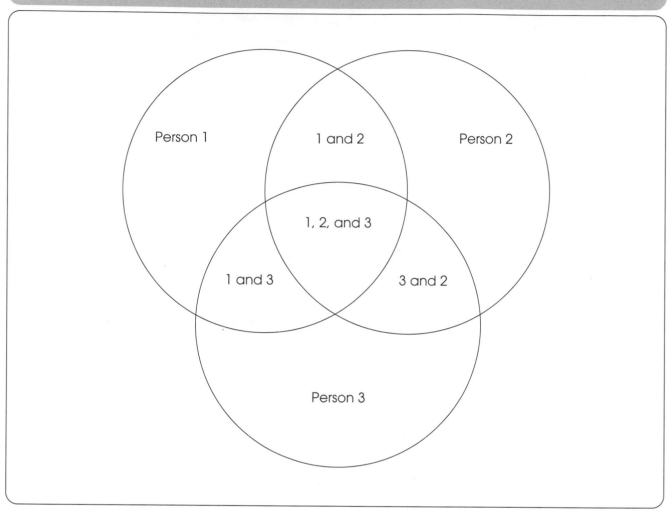

FIGURE 3.3—STATEMENT OF PURPOSE

School Support Teams (SSTs) will be powerful catalysts for significant change in our state's public schools. SSTs are not intended to monitor or investigate schools. They are intended to encourage schools to consider their own policies, programs, and practices in a manner that results in high-quality decision making about the need to continue, modify, or redirect efforts. SSTs are not intended to provide solutions or answers. Instead, they are expected to help schools grapple with difficult questions so that their capacity for solving educational problems is increased. SSTs are not intended to change schools; rather, they are intended to facilitate change by helping schools initiate and organize their own change efforts.

FIGURE 3.4—CASE STUDY FOR THE MONTROSE ELEMENTARY SCHOOL SUPPORT TEAM

You are the School Support Team for Montrose Elementary. The members of the Campus Leadership Team (CLT) who were elected by the faculty at Montrose include one department head (language arts), two grade level teachers (1st and 5th grade), one Title I teacher, one special education teachers (all grade levels), the counselor, the principal, and two parents: the business manager at the local grocery store (an adopter of the school) and a mother with four children attending Montrose.

Montrose Elementary School has 785 students enrolled. This school has had a small Title I program but is now eligible for a schoolwide program. The school consists of 26 percent European-American, 44 percent Latino, and 30 percent African-American students. The state's standardized criterion-referenced test revealed scores that, although low, have shown incremental gains in the last two years. Of the 3rd graders, fewer than 15 percent passed the math section, and fewer than 20 percent passed the reading section last year. In grade 5, fewer than 12 percent of the students passed the math section, fewer than 26 percent passed the reading section, but 59 percent passed the writing section on the standardized achievement test. No other assessments were used for 3rd or 5th grades, but the school used the Iowa Test of Basic Skills (ITBS) for all other grade levels except for kindergarten and 1st grade. The kindergarten and 1st grade teachers used a locally adopted checklist. Approximately 18 percent of the 1st grade students were recommended for retention, and 5 percent of the kindergarten students were recommended to repeat.

After a large housing project opened in the Montrose Elementary attendance zone, the number of students identified as economically disadvantaged jumped from 54 percent in 1993 to 78 percent in 1994. For the most part, the student population is very mobile, but with the new housing project it is hoped that the population will be more stable. The city has targeted this area as a high crime area and is providing increased police services. The city is also developing a community involvement project and is providing approximately $500,000 per year for summer youth programs and job development training.

You are attending the first meeting with the CLT. In your group, please discuss how you can support this school and other information you need to be effective. Next, identify the following for this school:

- Areas of possible strength
- Possible resources available
- Areas for growth for this school/community
- Questions that might assist the school community in examining its potential to help all students experience a love of learning and academic success.

Note: This case study was contributed by Darlene Yanez of the Charles A. Dana Center at the University of Texas at Austin. Montrose Elementary School is a fictitious name.

FIGURE 3.5—CASE STUDY ANALYSIS MATRIX

Strengths	Resources	Needs (Issues)	Needs Written as Answerable Questions (Visions)

In particular, attention will be focused toward identifying strengths, needs, and visions related to curriculum, instruction, and organization. *Note:* The focus is not on strengths, needs, and visions related exclusively to the Chapter 1/Title I program. Instead, focus should be on the entire school program and its influence on student involvement.

Participants with the numbers "1" and "3," form two separate subgroups and discuss

- What are the problems/obstacles to school reform?

- What are the implications of these obstacles for your role as a schoolwide reform facilitator?

- Given these obstacles, what strategies can you use to overcome these obstacles?

Participants with the numbers "2" and "4," form two separate subgroups and discuss

- What are the propositions for success to school reform?

- What are the implications of these propositions on your role as a schoolwide reform facilitator?

- What strategies can you use to maximize these propositions for success with schoolwide reform?

FIGURE 3.8—DEBRIEFING FOR SCHOOL REFORM JIGSAW ACTIVITY: GROUPS 1 AND 3

Challenging Issues/Circumstances

Ideas to Overcome Challenges

1.

1.

2.

2.

3.

3.

FIGURE 3.9—DEBRIEFING FOR SCHOOL REFORM JIGSAW ACTIVITY: GROUPS 2 AND 4

Insights about school reform:

Implications for your role as a schoolwide reform facilitator:

FIGURE 3.10—AGENDA FOR A SCHOOL SUPPORT TEAM VISIT

During the first full School Support Team visit, team members will

- Introduce themselves to the School Leadership Team (SLT) and any other school community members who are in attendance

- Facilitate an icebreaker activity

- Review an agenda (that was cooperatively constructed with the principal and SLT representatives at a pre-visit by the SST coordinator)

- Review a "campus portrait" that the school has prepared to highlight its many features. (This can be a portfolio, a scrapbook, a video, a collage, a CD Rom—and/or any other form of creating a picture of how the school community sees itself)

- Facilitate a dialogue about the campus's expectations of the School Support Team

- Review the campus plan and vision

- Facilitate a dialogue on campus priorities for continuous improvement

- Discuss any details of the day that need to be mentioned (e.g., when, where, and with whom the SST will eat lunch)

- Tour the campus and visit with staff, parents, students, and community members

- Conduct an exit meeting with the SLT, the principal, and any other interested school community members in order to (1) share experiences, (2) discuss the school's strengths, (3) further discuss its priorities for continuous improvement, (4) identify meaningful ways in which the SST can provide support (including short-term and long-range goals), (5) plan a second visit, and (6) facilitate a closure activity.

FIGURE 3.11—K-W-L PLANNING INSTRUMENT

What do we know?	What do we want to know?	With what we learned, how will we proceed?

FIGURE 3.12—CREATING A RESTRUCTURING AGREEMENT

1. We commit to using meaningful and comprehensive data to make decisions.

2. We commit to creating and sustaining a culture of continued self-examination, extensive and continual professional development, and experimentation.

3. We commit to accepting the challenge of helping *all* learners to succeed.

4. We commit to viewing children and youth as human beings first, students second.

5. We commit to learning and implementing a broad range of instructional methods and curricular materials.

6. We commit to discarding what doesn't work or is no longer relevant.

7. We commit to respecting parents, family, and community members as equal partners in the education of children.

8. We commit to creating opportunities for broad-based staff involvement in decision making clearly focused on change.

9. We commit to establishing a shared vision of education within the school.

10. We commit to assisting adults who are threatened or challenged by changes occurring in the school. In return, all adults in the school agree to be supportive or constructively critical.

Source: Adapted from D. T. Conley, (1993), *Roadmap to Restructuring: Policies, Practices, and the Emerging Values of Schooling,* (Eugene, Oreg.: ERIC Clearinghouse on Educational Management). Reprinted by permission of the publisher.

- Ask staff to identify with whom and when they need to collaborate, and redesign the master schedule to accommodate these needs.

- Hire "permanent substitutes" to rotate through classrooms to periodically free up teachers to attend meetings during the day rather than before or after school.

- Institute a community service component to the curriculum; when students are in the community (e.g., Thursday afternoon), teachers meet.

- Schedule "specials" (e.g., art, music, clubs, and tutorials) during the same time blocks (e.g., first and second period), so teachers have one or two hours a day to collaborate.

- Engage parents, family members, and community members to plan and conduct half-day or full-day exploratory, craft, hobby (e.g., gourmet cooking, puppetry, photography), theater, or other experiential programs.

- Partner with colleges and universities; have their faculty teach in the school, or offer distance learning lessons, demonstrations, and on-campus experiences to free up school personnel.

- Rearrange the school day to include a 50- to 60-minute block of time before or after school for collaborative meeting and planning.

- Lengthen the school day for students by 15 to 30 minutes. The cumulative "extra" student contact hours each month allow for periodic early dismissal of students and time for teachers to meet.

- Earmark some professional development days for collaborative meetings.

- Use faculty time for small-group meetings to solve problems related to issues of immediate and long-range importance.

- Build into the school schedule at least one "collaboration day" per marking period or month.

- Lengthen the school year for staff but not for students, or shorten the school year for students but not for staff.

- Go to year-round schooling with three-week breaks every quarter; devote four or five of the three-week intersession days to teacher collaboration.

Note: Parents and family members are frequently assumed to be opponents of scheduling changes. Schools that elicit support from parents and family members in planning needed changes, however, as well as schools that explain changes in terms of how students will benefit have reported widespread support for new ideas.

—From: R. A. Villa and J. S. Thousand, eds., (1995), *Creating an Inclusive School,* (Alexandria, Va.: Association for Supervision and Curriculum Development), p. 67. Copyright © 1995 by ASCD.

FIGURE 3.14—ACTION PLAN: PLANNING TO PLAN

School: _____ Date: _____

How will you solicit involvement in schoolwide planning from school staff, family members, and community members? _____
_____
_____

How might the core group find uninterrupted time to meet? _____
_____
_____

How might the core group solicit input from the school community in order to develop new ideas and commitment for helping all students experience academic success? _____
_____
_____

How will the core group keep members of the school community informed as planning progresses? _____
_____
_____

What resources might facilitate meaningful planning? _____
_____
_____

What kind of a timeline might help your school to accomplish its goals? _____
_____
_____

What roles might core planners accept in order to develop a comprehensive and substantive plan? (Roles should correspond to features of the timeline as well as to general needs such as who will prepare agendas for meetings, who will facilitate meetings, who will oversee communication with the school community, etc.) _____
_____
_____

How will your school ensure that decisions have a direct impact on teaching and learning?_____
_____
_____
_____

Figure 3.15—Reflection Log

Please complete each of the following in a sentence or two as you reflect on the exercise (or institute) in which you have just participated:

1. I learned . . .

2. I wonder . . .

3. I am surprised . . .

4. I wish . . .

5. I think . . .

6. I suggest . . .

because . . .

Source: B. K. Beyer. (1995). *How to Conduct a Formative Evaluation.* Alexandria, Va.: Association for Supervision and Curriculum Development, p. 46. Copyright © 1995 by Barry K. Beyer. Reprinted by permission.

FIGURE 3.16— HEAD, HEART, AND HAND ACTIVITY

HEAD (Thought):   One thing that I am *thinking* about as a consequence of participating in this activity (or institute) is . . .

HEART (Feelings):   One thing that I am *feeling* is . . .

HAND (Action):   One thing that I will *do* is . . .

4 Questions and Answers

When we first began to plan an approach to developing a system of school support teams, we formed study groups to examine questions on such topics as school change, external change agents, effective teams, and opportunities established in P.L.103-382, Section 1117 (c)(1), which addresses the school support team concept for Title I schools. This chapter addresses some basic questions we and others have raised. It also attempts to provide some guidance for understanding complex issues. Our responses are by no means exhaustive, and we encourage you to browse the Bibliography (p. 61) for more thorough reference materials.

382) provides a purpose in the context of Title I. Briefly, the purpose of school support teams is to work cooperatively with high-poverty (Title I) schools that are planning schoolwide programs, that are already schoolwide programs (because we know that school improvement is an ongoing process), or that are identified as being in need of improvement. The results of this cooperative venture ought to be increased opportunity for all students to meet a state's content standards and student performance standards. For the complete text of Section 1117 (and portions of Sections 1114 and 1115), see Appendix A.

What Is the Purpose of School Support Teams?

The purpose of SSTs is to support a school through the challenging process of constructive change in a way that leads a school to define and actualize its own vision that includes high achievement for every student. The legislation (Section 1117 of P.L. 103-

Who Might Participate on a School Support Team?

SST members include distinguished and experienced educators from kindergarten through postsecondary education, as well as other professionals, parents, and community members who are knowledgeable about school change. Optimally, school support teams will be composed of members from a range of cultural and ethnic communities to expand perspectives on the opportunities for all students. The following are additional possibilities: retired educators, regional educational cooperatives or service center staff, vocational technical personnel, students, business leaders, chamber of commerce staff, job service personnel, and law enforcement personnel.

How Many People Should Serve on an SST, and How Many Visits Should a School Receive?

Neither the legislation nor our experience specifies an optimal number of participants for each team or an optimal number of visits. The number of team members and the frequency of service ought to be determined cooperatively between the school support team leader (or representative) and the school principal, and, if applicable, the site-based decision-making team. The goal is to increase the opportunity for all students to meet a state's content standards and student performance standards. Therefore, the design of assistance will be collectively determined by the SST leader and the school. Here are two examples.

1. A school requests assistance in planning its schoolwide program. On the first visit, an SST member works with the school to decide the type of support that would be most beneficial toward increasing the performance levels of the students. On the second SST visit, five people assist different content-area planning groups. On the third visit, two members conduct a follow-up meeting with the site-based decision-making team's math subgroup. At the end of the visit, SST members, in cooperation with school representatives, determine that over the next month, assistance will by phone, fax, and e-mail.

2. A school has been working on its plan for a year and has received excellent ratings on the achievement of its students. When offered the assistance of an SST, the school principal meets with the site-based decision-making team and determines that very little assistance is needed. Even though the school's students are experiencing general success, however, school staff request an SST composed of a principal and teacher from outside of the school to recommend how they might build on the strengths of their plan. At the end of the visit, the two SST members, in cooperation with school representatives, determine that future assistance will be by request.

What Are the Benefits for School Support Team Members?

The SST experience

- Provides professional development growth opportunities;
- Provides the opportunity to network with other educators committed to school change and exemplary teaching and learning;
- Provides professional development in facilitation, team collaboration, and problem solving;
- Strengthens skills in interpersonal relations and group processing skills; and
- Revives hope.

What Is a Practical Resource for Understanding, Planning, and Implementing Schoolwide Programs?

As a start, we recommend *An Idea Book: Implementing Schoolwide Programs,* a publication of the United States Department of Education (Pechman and Feister 1994). It explains (1) the rationale for schoolwide programs; (2) the evolution of schoolwide programs; (3) information on successful schoolwide leadership, planning, academic issues, and instructional flexibility; (4) promising practices and a delineation of key features of successful schoolwide programs; (5) challenges and opportunities, including the need to move beyond reduced class size; (6)

profiles of effective schoolwide programs; (7) planning resources; and (8) references. The Title I office at State Departments of Education can also provide information and references that may be useful. In addition, we encourage you to review the Bibliography (p. 61).

What Goals Might a School Support Team Set?

Specific goals vary according to the needs of the school that is being served. General goals include:

• Develop trust between team members and members of the school community: *Trust must be established for feedback to be effectively given and received.*

• Facilitate learning: *Members of the school community ought to be able to learn new and important things about themselves, their potential, and exciting opportunities in a way that allows them to think and act differently than when the SST process first began.*

• Assist a school in developing autonomy as a reflective, action-oriented community: *Members of the school community should reach a high-level of self-awareness and confidence that allows them to design their own facilitation and school change processes.*

What Caveats Should SST Members Consider Before Becoming Change Agents

The work of Carl Glickman, Richard Hayes, and Frances Hensley (1992) with the League of Professional Schools (Appendix Q) affirms our experience that

• Conflict will increase when members of shared governance teams take their responsibilities seriously;

• Assessment information will cultivate dissatisfaction and possibly blame if student learning and attitudes do not match with "the cardiac approach" to believing that "in our hearts we're doing fine" (Wolfe 1969);

• Without new information, decisions will be made that reinforce the status quo;

• With immediate school success, pressure for more short-term success will increase at the potential cost of long-term student gains;

• Decisions about dreams will be easier than decisions about how to attain one's dreams; and

• Criticism will develop from the outside, especially as a school attains success and recognition.

What Does the Future Hold?

Of course, there are no crystal balls. And in spite of our respect for human empathy, insight, imagination, and energy, we must accept that there are no panaceas, only opportunities. School change is a complex, nonlinear process that requires a continuous, open exchange of information, resources, model practices, and ideas; participation from as many representatives of the school community as possible; validation of important work; planning time as a part of everyday work; and support at all levels within a school district.

As the world, communities, organizations, and schools move toward interdependence, there is still a lot to learn about collaborating in ways that support a shared sense of dignity and hope. But we are becoming stronger in understanding that unification of purpose and shared responsibility can feed the sources of motivation in all of us—SST members, school-based educators, and students. Our greatest hope is that we continue to catalyze this motivation so that our children are able to understand one of life's most important lessons: education and concern for others are inseparable ideals.

Bibliography

Allen, L., and B. Lunsford. (1995). *How to Form Networks for School Renewal.* Alexandria, Va.: Association for Supervision and Curriculum Development.

Apple, M. W., and J. A. Beane, eds. (1995). *Democratic Schools.* Alexandria, Va.: Association for Supervision and Curriculum Development.

Beyer, B. K. (1995). *How to Conduct a Formative Evaluation.* Alexandria, Va.: Association for Supervision and Curriculum Development.

Brandt, R. (November 1995). "On Restructuring Schools: A Conversation with Fred Newmann." *Educational Leadership* 53, 3: 70–73.

Bryk, A. S., et al. (September 1994). "The State of Chicago School Reform." *Phi Delta Kappan* 76: 74–78.

Conley, D. T. (1993). *Roadmap to Restructuring: Policies, Practices, and the Emerging Values of Schooling.* Eugene, Oreg.: ERIC Clearinghouse on Educational Management.

Costa, A. L., and B. Kallick. (October 1993). "Through the Lens of a Critical Friend." *Educational Leadership* 51, 2: 49–51.

Cranton, P. (1996). *Professional Development as Transformative Learning: New Perspectives for Teachers of Adults.* San Francisco: Jossey Bass.

Cummins, J. (1986). "Empowering Minority Students: A Framework for Intervention." Harvard *Educational Review* 56, 1: 18–36.

Francis, S., S. Hirsh, and E. Rowland. (Spring 1994). "Improving School Culture Through Study Groups." *Journal of Staff Development* 15, 2.

Fullan, M., and M. Miles. (June 1992). "Getting Reform Right: What Works and What Doesn't." *Phi Delta Kappan* 73, 10: 745–752.

Gardner, H. (1993). *Multiple Intelligences: The Theory in Practice.* New York: Basic Books.

Ginsberg, M., and A. B. Anderson. (August 1995). *Texas School Support Team Pilot Initiative: Evaluation Report.* Denver, Colo.: Region E Technical Assistance Center, RMC Research Corporation.

Ginsberg, M., and J. Johnson. (October 1995). "Designing and Implementing School Support Teams: Notes from the Field." Unpublished manuscript, Region E Technical Assistance Center, Denver, Colo.

Glickman, C. D., L. Allen, and B. F. Lundsford. (Summer 1994). "Factors Affecting School Change." *Journal of Professional Development* 15, 3.

Glickman, C. D., R. Hayes, and F. Hensley. (Spring 1992). "Site-Based Facilitation of Empowered Schools: Complexities and Issues for Staff Developers." *Journal of Staff Development* 13, 2: 22–26.

Hargreaves, A. (1994). *Changing Teachers, Changing Times: Teachers' Work and Culture in the Postmodern Age.* New York: Teachers College Press.

Johnson, J. F., Jr., and M. Ginsberg. (November 1996). "Building Capacity Through School Support Teams." *Educational Leadership* 54, 3: 80–82.

Lasoff, M., L. Olson, and M. Sommerfield. "School-Reform Networks at a Glance." (November 2, 1994). *Education Week* 14, 9: 34-41.

Lein, L. J. Johnson, M. Ragland, et al. (1996). "Successful Texas Schoolwide Programs." Unpublished manuscript, The Charles A. Dana Center, University of Texas at Austin.

Levin, H. M. (1988). *Accelerated Schools for At-Risk Students.* New Brunswick, N.J.: Center for Policy Research in Education.

Levin, H. M., and W. S. Hopfenberg. (January 1991). "Don't Remediate: Accelerate!" *Principal* 70: 11-13.

Lieberman, A., and M. Grolnick. (1997). "Networks, Reform, and the Professional Development of Teachers." In *Rethinking Educational Change with Heart and Mind. 1997 ASCD Yearbook,* edited by Andy Hargreaves, pp. 192-215. Alexandria, Va.: Association for Supervision and Curriculum Development.

Lieberman, A., and M. McLaughlin. (1992). "Networks for Educational Change: Powerful and Problematic." *Phi Delta Kappan* 73, 9: 673–677.

Lindle, J. C., B. S. Gale, and B. S. Curry-White. (1994). *School Based Decision Making: 1994 Survey.* Frankfort: Kentucky Department of Education and the University of Kentucky/University of Louisville Joint Center for the Study of Educational Policy and the Kentucky Institute for Education Research.

McLaughlin, M. W. (December 1990). "The Rand Change Agency Study Revisited: Macro Perspectives and Micro Realities." *Educational Researcher* 11–16.

Miles, M. B., E. R. Saxl, and A. Lieberman. (1988). "What Skills Do Educational 'Change Agents' Need? An Empirical View." *Curriculum Inquiry* 18: 2: 157-193.

Moffet, C. (Winter 1996). "School Support Teams: Facilitating Success in High-Poverty Schools." *ASCD Professional Development Newsletter:* 1-2, 8 (published by the Association for Supervision and Curriculum Development, Alexandria, Va.).

Ogle, D. (1986). "K-W-L.: A Teaching Model That Develops Active Reading of Expository Text." *The Reading Teacher* 39: 564–576.

Pechman, E. M., and L. Feister, Policy Studies Institute. (May 1994). *An Idea Book: Implementing Schoolwide Programs.* Washington, D.C.: United States Department of Education.

Public Law 103-382. (1994). Improving America's Schools Act. Section 1117c.

Saxl, E. R., with M. B. Miles and A. Lieberman. (1989). *Assisting Change in Education.* New York: Center for Policy Research; Seattle: University of Washington; Alexandria, Va.: Association for Supervision and Curriculum Development.

Saxl, E. R., with M. B. Miles and A. Lieberman. (1989). *Assisting Change in Education Trainer's Manual.* New York: Center for Policy Research; Seattle: University of Washington; Alexandria, Va.: Association for Supervision and Curriculum Development.

Schenck, E. A., and S. Beckstrom. (1993). *Chapter I Schoolwide Project Study, Final Report.* Portsmouth, N.H.: RMC Research.

Senge, P. M. (1990). *The Fifth Discipline: The Art and Practice of the Learning Organization.* New York: Doubleday.

Slavin, R. E., N. L. Karweit, and B. A. Wasik. (1994). *Preventing Early School Failure.* Boston: Allyn and Bacon.

Smylie, M. A. (1994). "Redesigning Teachers' Work: Connections to the Classroom." In *Review of Research in Education,* edited by L. Darling–Hammond. Washington, D.C.: American Educational Research Association.

Sparks, D. (1995). "A Paradigm Shift in Staff Development." *The ERIC Review*: 2–4.

U.S. Department of Education. (February 1993). *Reinventing Chapter I: The Current Chapter I Program and New Directions, Final Report of the National Assessment of Chapter I Program.* Washington, D.C.: U.S. Department of Education.

Villa, R. A., and J. S. Thousand, eds. (1995). *Creating an Inclusive School.* Alexandria, Va.: Association for Supervision and Curriculum Development.

Weiss, C. H. (Fall 1993). "Shared Decision Making About What? A Comparison of Schools With and Without Teacher Participation." *Teachers College Record* 93, 1: 69–92.

Wlodkowski, R. J., and M. B. Ginsberg. (1995). *Diversity and Motivation: Culturally Responsive Teaching.* San Francisco: Jossey–Bass, Inc.

Wolfe, R. (1969). "A Model for Curriculum Evaluation." *Psychology in the Schools* 6: 107–108.

TITLE I LEGISLATIVE SUMMARY

Important Points of Section 1117 School Support Team Requirements

Section 1117—Requires states to develop systems for school support and improvement.

• States must establish a statewide system of intensive and sustained support for schoolwide programs and schools in need of program improvement.

Funds reserved under Section 1003a (0.5 percent of Title I funds allocated to the state) or funds allocated under Section 1002f (program improvement funds) are to be used to develop and implement the statewide system of support. States may also use state administrative Title I funds for this purpose.

• The statewide support system must work with and receive support and assistance from the comprehensive regional technical assistance centers (to be established under contract from the U.S. Department of Education) and the regional education laboratories.

The system shall minimally include the development of a school support team system, the identification of distinguished schools, and assistance from distinguished educators.

School Support Teams

• A system of school support teams must be established by the state in consultation with districts and campuses. The school support teams are to assist
  — schools planning or implementing schoolwide programs, and if funds are sufficient;
  — schools in which 75% or more of the students meet poverty criteria;
  — schools in the school improvement process as required by Section 1116; and
  — other schools in need of improvement.

• School support teams shall be composed of teachers, pupil services personnel, distinguished educators (as described below) and others who are knowledgeable about research on teaching, teaming, and school reform (e.g., representatives of institutions of higher education, regional education laboratories, and outside consultant groups).

The school support teams shall work cooperatively with schools to make recommendations as schoolwide program plans or school improvement plans are developed and implemented.

During the implementation of the schoolwide program plan or school improvement plan, the school support teams shall
  — periodically review campus progress;
  — identify problems in the design and operation of the instructional program; and
  — make recommendations for improvement to the school and the school district.

Distinguished Schools

Schools shall be designated as distinguished schools if
  — for three consecutive years, the school has exceeded the state's standard of adequate yearly progress as defined in the state plan; or
  — virtually all students have met the state's advanced level of student performance (as defined in the state plan) and equity in participation and achievement of students by gender has been achieved or significantly improved.

Distinguished schools may serve as models and provide support to other schools, especially schoolwide programs and schools in school improvement.

- States shall use funds reserved under Section 1003a (0.5 percent of Title I funds allocated to the state) or funds allocated under Section 1002f (program improvement funds) to
  — allow distinguished schools to provide assistance to other schools; and
  — to provide awards to distinguished schools.

Awards provided to distinguished schools may be used to further the school's education programs or reward individuals or groups for exemplary performance.

- School districts may use Title I, Part A funds to provide additional rewards to distinguished schools. Such rewards may include:
  — greater decision-making authority at the school building level;
  — increased access to resources or supplemental services (e.g., summer school);
  — additional professional development opportunities;
  — opportunities to participate in special projects; and
  — individual financial bonuses.

Distinguished Educators

The state shall establish a corps of distinguished educators using funds reserved under Section 1003a (0.5 percent of Title I funds allocated to the state) or funds allocated under Section 1002f (program improvement funds). Funds may be used for release time, travel, training, and other related costs.

- When possible, distinguished educators shall be chosen from Title I schools that have been especially successful in helping children meet the state performance standards (such as distinguished schools).

Distinguished educators shall provide intensive and sustained assistance to schools and school districts farthest from meeting the state's performance

standards and to schoolwide programs. This assistance may be provided through participation in school support teams.

Alternatives

The state may devise additional approaches to providing assistance such as would be provided by school support teams or distinguished educators. Alternatives such as the use of education service centers or institutions of higher education would have to be approved by the Secretary of Education in the state plan.

Important Points of Section 1114 Schoolwide Program Requirements Reauthorization of Title I Elementary and Secondary Education Act

Part A   Improving Basic Programs operated by
         Local Education Agencies
         September 1994

Section 1114—Describes schoolwide program requirements.

Campus Eligibility

In the 1995–96 school year, schools may become schoolwide programs if 60 percent or more of the children in the attendance area or enrolled in the school are from families that meet the district's low-income criteria.

In the 1996–97 school year (and all subsequent years), schools may become schoolwide programs if 50 percent or more of the children in the attendance area or enrolled in the school are from families that meet the district's low-income criteria.

School districts may begin new schoolwide programs after the state establishes a system of school support teams. Prior to the development of a school support team system, to become schoolwide programs, campuses must demonstrate to their school district that they have received high-quality technical assistance in the development of their schoolwide program plans.

For schools that are currently operating a schoolwide project, schools may continue to operate such programs provided that during the 1995–96 school year, a new plan is developed reflecting all of the provisions of the new law.

Inclusion of Other Federal Programs in Schoolwide Programs

The U.S. Secretary of Education may exempt schoolwide programs for statutory or regulatory provisions for other federal formula or discretionary programs so that those programs may support schoolwide program efforts if the intent and purposes of the other programs are met. (Excludes programs under the Individuals with Disabilities in Education Act.)

Schoolwide programs that use funds from other federal programs in support of the schoolwide program are not relieved of requirements relating to health, safety, civil rights, gender equity, student and parent participation and involvement, services to private school children, maintenance of effort, comparability of services, or the use of federal funds to supplement, not supplant.

Use of Funds

School districts can use Title I funds in combination with other federal, state, and local funds to upgrade the entire educational program of schoolwide program campuses.

Schoolwide programs will not be required to identify any child as eligible to participate in the schoolwide program or to receive supplemental services; thus, funds can be used to benefit each child enrolled on the schoolwide program campus.

Schoolwide programs must use funds to supplement non-federal fund sources that are available to the school.

Schoolwide programs must devote sufficient resources to carry out professional development activities for teachers, aides and, where appropriate, pupil services personnel, parents, principals, and other school personnel.

Development of the Schoolwide Program Plan

Any eligible school that wants to become a schoolwide program shall develop (or amend) , in consultation with the school district, and the campus, school support team or other technical assistance provider, a comprehensive plan for reforming the total instructional program in the school. The plan must include all of the components listed below.

The schoolwide program plan shall be developed during a one-year period unless the school district, after considering the recommendations of technical assistance providers, determines that less time is needed to develop and implement a plan.

The schoolwide program plan must be developed with the involvement of the community to be served and the individuals who will carry out the plan, including teachers, principals, support staff, parents, and students (if a secondary school).

If the schoolwide program plan is not satisfactory to the parents of children enrolled at the school, the school must submit any parent comments on the plan to the school district when the school makes the plan available to the school district.

Contents of the Schoolwide Program Plan

The schoolwide program plan must list all of the other federal, state, and local programs that will be included in the schoolwide program and describe how the school will use resources from Title I, Part A with the other resources to implement all of the components listed above.

Schoolwide programs must include a comprehensive needs assessment of the entire school based on performance data related to the state content and performance standards.

Schoolwide programs must include schoolwide reform strategies that provide all children opportunities to meet state performance standards and are based on effective means of improving achievement.

Schoolwide programs may use instructional strategies that

— increase the amount and quality of learning time;
— provide enriched and accelerated curricula;
— include strategies for meeting the needs of historically underserved populations (including the incorporation of gender-equitable methods and practices); and
— address the needs of all children, but particularly the needs of children who are members of the target population of any program included in the schoolwide program.

Schoolwide program instructional strategies may include the integration of vocational and academic learning, applied learning, and team teaching.

Schoolwide programs must address student needs through services that may include counseling pupil services, mentor services, college and career awareness and preparation, or services to prepare students for the transition from school-to-work.

Schoolwide program plans must address how the school will determine if student needs have been met.

In schoolwide programs, instruction must be provided by highly qualified professional staff. (See

Section 1119 regarding the employment of instructional aides.)

Schoolwide programs must have strategies for improving parental involvement, such as family literacy services.

Schoolwide programs must have plans for assisting preschool children in the transition from early childhood programs such as Head Start, Even Start, or state-funded preschool programs to elementary school programs.

Schoolwide programs must have strategies for including teachers in the decisions regarding the use of any additional assessments (beyond those required in the state plan) that are part of the school district's Title I plan.

The schoolwide program plan must describe how the school will provide individual student assessment results, including an interpretation of those results, to the parents of children who participate in the assessment program.

Schoolwide programs must have provisions to offer timely additional assistance to children who, during the course of the school year, experience difficulty in achieving the state content and performance standards. Such provisions shall include:

— systems for ensuring that student difficulties are identified on a timely basis;
— periodic training for teachers in how to identify such difficulties and provide assistance to individual students (to the extent the school determines feasible)
— teacher-parent conferences that include discussions of what the school will do to help the student meet state content and performance standards, what parents can do to help their children meet those standards, and what additional assistance may be available at school or in the community.

The schoolwide program plan must describe how the school will disaggregate assessment results by gender, major ethnic/racial groups, socioeconomic status, and limited English proficiency status. Additionally, the results must be disaggregated to determine the performance of students who are migratory and children with disabilities. The plan must describe how the school will seek to produce statistically sound results for each category for which assessment results are disaggregated and provide public reporting of the data only when such reporting is statistically sound.

The schoolwide program plan shall be in effect for the duration of the school's participation in Title I. It shall be reviewed and revised as necessary.

The schoolwide program plan shall be made available to the school district, parents, and the public. The contents of the plan shall be translated (to the extent feasible) into any language spoken as a primary language by a significant percentage of the parents of the school's students.

The schoolwide program plan (where appropriate) should be coordinated with programs under the School-to-Work Opportunities Act, the Perkins Vocational and Applied Technology Act, and the National Community Service Act.

The schoolwide program is subject to the school improvement provisions of Section 1116.

Section 1115—Describes targeted assistance schools.

All schools receiving Title I, Part A funds that are ineligible to be schoolwide programs, or choose not to be schoolwide programs must use Title I, Part A funds for programs that provide services to eligible children identified as having the greatest need for special services.

Student Eligibility

Children who at any time in the preceding two years participated in Head Start or Even Start;

Children who at any time in the preceding two years received services for youth who are neglected or delinquent;

Children who are homeless; or

Children living in facilities for youth who are neglected or delinquent.

Children with disabilities, with limited English proficiency, children from migratory families, and children whose families meet low-income criteria shall be eligible for services on the same basis as other children selected to receive services.

Use of Funds

Funds may not be used to provide services that are otherwise required by law to be made available; but may be used to coordinate or supplement such services for eligible children.

Targeted assistance programs must use Title I, Part A resources to assist children who are eligible for participation in the program meet the state's student performance standards.

To be eligible, children must meet the following criteria: be of legal school age or younger if at an age where they can benefit from an organized instructional program provided in a school or other educational setting; be identified by the school as failing to meet the state's student performance standards or most at risk of failing to meet those standards. Students must be identified on the basis of multiple, educationally related, objective criteria established by the district and supplemented by the school.

Children from preschool ages through grade two shall be identified only through methods such as teacher judgment, interviews with parents, and developmentally appropriate criteria.

Additionally, children who meet any of the following criteria shall be considered eligible: children who at any time in the preceding two years participated in Head Start or Even Start programs; children who are experiencing homelessness (even if they do not attend a school designated as a Title I school); children who are neglected or delinquent and either reside in facilities or attend community day programs for such children; and children who, at any time during the previous two years, received services from Title I, Part D programs designed to serve students who are neglected or delinquent. Targeted assistance programs are to be designed in a manner that helps these eligible children meet the state student performance standards.

Targeted assistance programs must set aside sufficient funds for professional development activities as required by Section 1119; however, schools may enter into consortia to facilitate meeting these requirements.

Targeted assistance programs must provide instruction by highly qualified staff. (See Section 1119 concerning the employment of instructional aides.)

Personnel funded by targeted assistance programs may
— assume limited duties assigned to similar personnel;
— participate in general professional development and school planning activities; and
— collaboratively teach with regular classroom teachers if such collaboration directly benefits participating children.

Targeted assistance programs must include strategies for increasing parental involvement, such as family literacy services.

Planning

Targeted assistance programs must be designed based on effective means for improving achievement.

The planning of targeted assistance programs must be incorporated into existing school planning efforts.

Instructional Strategies

Targeted assistance programs must use effective instructional strategies that
— give primary consideration to providing extended learning time (e.g., extended year, extended day) opportunities;
— help provide an accelerated, high-quality curriculum, including applied learning; and
— minimize removing children from the regular classroom during regular school hours.

Targeted assistance programs must coordinate with and support the regular program through activities which may include:
— counseling, mentoring, and other pupil services;
— college and career awareness and preparation;
— services to prepare students from the transition from school to work;
— services to assist preschool children in the transition from early childhood programs to elementary school.

Targeted assistance programs must provide opportunities for professional development for administrators, teachers, and other school staff who work with participating children either in Title I programs or in regular education programs.

Targeted assistance programs must help participating children meet state performance standards by
— coordinating Title I, Part A resources with other resources, and

— reviewing the progress of participating children and revising the program to provide additional assistance if necessary.

Targeted assistance programs may serve participating students simultaneously with other students with similar needs in the same educational settings where appropriate.

If health, nutrition, and social services are not otherwise available, yet have been identified as necessary through a comprehensive needs assessment, and collaborative partnerships have been established with local service providers, then a portion of the Title I, Part A funds may be used as a last resort to provide such services including:

— the provision of basic medical equipment such as eyeglasses and hearing aids;
— compensation of a coordinator, and
— professional development to assist teachers, pupil services personnel, other staff, and parents.

OVERHEADS: EFFECTIVE SCHOOLWIDE PROGRAMS

O V E R H E A D 1

COMMON FEATURES:

- An agreed-upon vision for all students, based on higher academic standards and adequate designs and plans to implement the vision

- A clear focus on academic achievement

- Extended planning and a collaborative design

- A well-defined structure for ensuring collaboration in planning, organizing, evaluating, and improving curriculum, instruction, and the organization of the school

- A community in which educators are continuously engaged in the process of learning to improve the effectiveness of their school

- Cultural inclusiveness

- Parent, family, and community involvement

- Evidence of student and school success

RECOMMENDED STEPS IN SCHOOLWIDE PLANNING

1. Establish a planning team.

2. Determine how the planning team will consistently communicate with the school community.

3. Conduct a comprehensive assessment of strengths and needs.

4. Organize the assessment data into a school profile.

5. Investigate the research base.

6. Draft comprehensive goals and specific objectives.

7. Incorporate research into the plan.

8. Review and modify the draft plan.

9. Complete the final plan.

EFFECTIVE SCHOOLWIDE PROGRAMS: CHALLENGES

- Adequate time to learn new roles

- Communication and involvement

- Moving beyond reduced class size

- Adequate preparation for new resources

- Including parents and the community

- Achievement variability

- Stabilizing change

- More progress in elementary schools

STATE-LEVEL LETTER OF INTRODUCTION

[Letterhead]

[Date]

[Name]
Department of Education
[University]
[Address]
[City], [State] [ZIP]

SUBJECT: Request for Nominations for Participants for [State] Chapter 1 School Support

Dear [Name]:

Our state is striving to implement the newly reauthorized Title I of the Elementary and Secondary Education ACT (ESEA), which provides more schools greater flexibility through the use of schoolwide program designs. Also, the new law intends to provide new structures to build the capacity of schools that have not yet attained the level of academic success they are capable of attaining. As a part of these changes, the new law allows for the creation of school support teams, whose purpose is to offer support and assistance in planning schoolwide programs and in campus program improvement efforts. The Division of School Improvement is implementing [number] school support team pilot sites this year to be better prepared for full-scale implementation next year. This letter is to request nominations from your college of education staff for participants on these pilot support teams.

We have asked [number] geographically and demographically diverse campuses to volunteer as pilot campuses. All are either current Title I schoolwide programs or are eligible to become schoolwide programs under the new laws. (These are schools with high concentrations of children whose families meet low-income criteria.) Furthermore, they are campuses where fewer than 10 percent of the students participating in the Title I program passed the [Texas Assessment of Academic Skills (TAAS)] last year. Additionally, all of the schools are involved in the Title I Campus Improvement Process. We felt that these campuses might have the most to gain from this pilot opportunity.

To make the support teams truly helpful to the pilot campuses, we are seeking a pool of potential support team members from education service centers and colleges of education, as well as administrators, teachers, and support personnel from schools where a high percentage of the students who participated in the Title I program passed all sections of the [TAAS]. All of the members will receive training in the support team processes. In particular, team members will come to understand that their role is not to monitor or dictate solutions but, rather, to help the school engage in a planning process that will lead to improved student achievement. Along with people who have experience in developing and implementing excellent Title I programs, the school support team should include others who are knowledgeable in working with groups on school reform, teaching and learning strategies, techniques for site-based decision making, and assessment/evaluation alternatives. Therefore, you are invited to nominate one or more candidates to participate in this school support team pilot.

A two-day training for selected pilot team members will occur on _____ at the _____ in _____. Each team member will be asked to participate on one or two support teams. The teams will visit their assigned campuses twice. The first meeting, in _____, will focus on planning for the use of Title I resources to improve achievement for all students, especially those who have not passed all sections of the [TAAS], or who may be expected to have difficulty in passing the test. Attention will be given to reviewing performance data, identifying strengths and needs, and considering options.

A follow-up meeting will be planned for _____. During the interim between the meetings, school support team members will be available for telephone consultation on planning questions or strategies. The follow-up meeting is intended to help the school continue a data-driven planning process.

For nominations to be considered, each candidate must have the approval of his or her dean or the dean's designee. The college of education must agree to provide travel, per diem, and release costs for attendance at the two-day training as well as for the two site visits. The nomination form is attached.* We believe this pilot will benefit both the recipients of the support as well as the support givers. Through this experience, we may all learn more about helping schools improve.

Sincerely,

[Name]
Senior Director
Division of School Improvement

*Authors' note: For sample forms referred to above, please see Figure 2.1 and Appendix E.

REGIONAL- OR DISTRICT-LEVEL LETTER OF INTRODUCTION

[Letterhead]

TO: [Administrator]

FROM: Coordinator of the Region _____ School Support Team

DATE: _____

SUBJECT: Nominations for the Region _____ School Support Team

As you may be aware, to receive federal funding for Title I, Part A of the Elementary and Secondary Act, as amended by the Improving America's Schools Act of 1994, all state agencies were mandated to include in their state plans a system of support for schools receiving funds under this part. In its efforts to conceptualize how this system of support might work, the [Texas Education Agency Division of Accelerated Instruction] conducted a pilot school support team (SST) during the _____ semester. Then, to serve local districts more effectively and efficiently, [TEA] entered into an agreement with the regional service centers for the centers to maintain this system of support. In early _____, [TEA] forwarded notification of this agreement to all school districts.

To provide support to Title I schools in accordance with the law, the Region _____ Education Service Center is now soliciting nominations for membership to the Region _____ School Support Team (SST). We hope that you will support our efforts to provide quality assistance by nominating persons from your staff, and possibly yourself.

Evaluation of the state's pilot SST indicates that members—exemplary classroom educators and experienced administrators from across the state, ESC staff, post-secondary faculty, and technical assistance personnel from research entities such as Southwest Educational Development Laboratory and RMC Research Corporation—benefited from the experience, as did the campus administrators and site teams of those campuses that participated in the pilot. Specifically, members of the pilot school support team grew professionally as a result of facilitating and engaging in creative decision-making processes with the school site teams and of developing informative collaborative relationships with one another.

Please find enclosed one nomination form, which we invite you to duplicate it to include as many nominees as you feel might well serve the SST.* We remind you that SST nominees should include classroom teachers, pupil services personnel, and/or administrative personnel. Also, we encourage the nominee to include any additional information relevant to his or her selection for SST membership. Please understand, however, that this information is *not* required. Please fax or mail the completed forms (including signatures of the nominee, his or her supervisor, and the superintendent) to me by _____.

The first day of training for SST members will occur _____, from _____ a.m. to _____ p.m. at _____. After the training, the Region _____ SST will be available to lend assistance to Title I campuses as outlined in the law, with the first priority being given to existing schoolwide programs (of which Region _____ now has _____), the second priority to campuses with 75 percent or greater low-SES student population, and finally to other Title I campuses. We have tentatively scheduled a second day of training during _____, and we may include a third day in _____ or _____, depending on the needs of the SST members. We ask that your district allow each of your SST members to make two on-site campus visits.

To fulfill the Region _____ School Support Team vision—providing educator-to-educator assistance so that Title I campuses "do things better for all students"—we urge you to submit your nominations.

We sincerely appreciate your support of and participation in this exciting endeavor.

Authors' note: For sample forms, please see Figure 2.1 and Appendix E.

NOMINATION FORM FOR SCHOOL SUPPORT TEAM MEMBERS

School district/educational institution _____ Campus/department _____

Name of nominee _____

Nominee's address _____

Phone number(s) where nominee can be contacted _____ Fax _____

Nominee's position/title _____

Nominee's grade-level experience(s) _____

Please check the area(s) that indicate nominee's experience in working with adult groups:

❑ Elementary school staff   ❑ Middle school staff   ❑ High school staff

❑ College students   ❑ Community members   ❑ Parents   ❑ School volunteers

Please check the area(s) in which the nominee has had successful experiences or area(s) in which he or she exhibits strengths:

❑   1. Campus improvement planning/schoolwide program planning

❑   2. Working with students in at-risk situations

❑   3. Chapter 1/Title I programs and services

❑   4. Instructional strategies in reading

❑   5. Instructional strategies in math

❑   6. Education of culturally diverse students and/or LEP students

❑   7. Assessment and evaluation

❑   8. Group change processes

❑   9. Site-based decision making/group decision making

❑ 10. Implementing innovative/new instructional programs

❑ 11. Building interpersonal relationships/team-building

❑ 12. Building parent/community involvement in school

❑ 13. Openness to varied/new instructional strategies and/or program design

Please add any information that will be useful in selecting this nominee for membership on a school support team. _____

_____

_____

I agree to (1) attend three days of training at _____; (2) participate in two visits of campuses outside my district; and (3) provide my own transportation to the campus(es) I will visit. ❑ Yes   ❑ No

Nominee's signature _____ Date _____

Supervisor's signature _____ Date _____

Superintendent's signature _____ Date _____

Note: We *invite* and *encourage* the nominee to share additional information he or she may wish to include on an additional page to be attached to this nomination form.

RESPONSE FORM FOR PARTICIPATION ON A SCHOOL SUPPORT TEAM

As a nominee for the Regional _____ School Support Team, please complete this form with the appropriate information and signatures:

I agree to attend one day of training at _____   ❑ Yes   ❑ No

I will be able to make 3–4 site visits to campuses in my region   ❑ Yes   ❑ No

Nominee's signature _____   Date _____

Supervisor's signature _____   Date _____

COORDINATING THE WORK OF SCHOOL SUPPORT TEAMS DIAGRAM

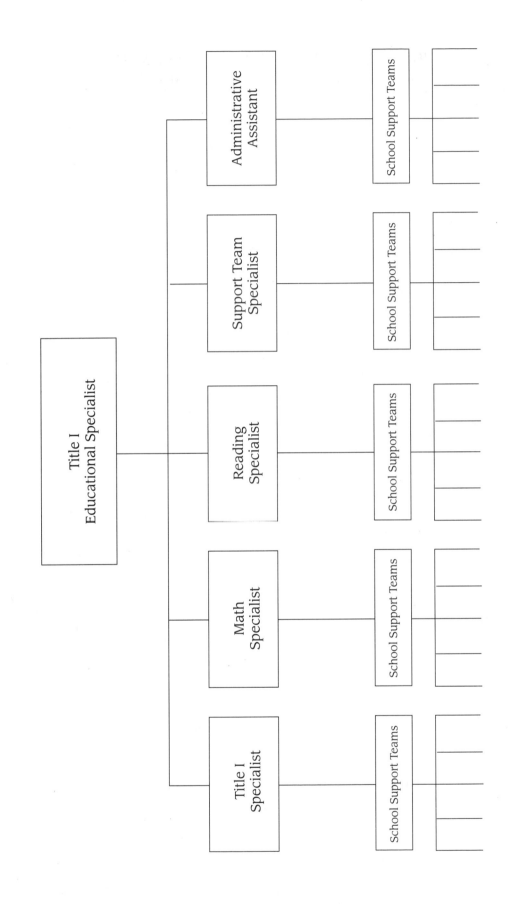

TITLE I SCHOOLWIDE PROGRAM PLANNING
SCHOOL SUPPORT TEAM REQUEST FORM

[Letterhead]

EDUCATION SERVICE CENTER ■ REGION _____

Please check the following as needed:

❑ **We request a School Support Team for**

    ❑ *Development of a Title I Schoolwide Plan*

    ❑ *Review of our Title I Schoolwide Program already in place*

    ❑ *Assistance with our Title I Schoolwide Program in the area(s) of*

        ❑ Curriculum

        ❑ Materials

        ❑ Instructional strategies

        ❑ Parental involvement

        ❑ Other _____

Please mail or fax questionnaire to:
[Name]
[Address]
[Fax number]

If you have any questions, you may contact me at _____.

❑ **We are moving forward with our Title I Schoolwide Program and do not need a visit from a School Support Team at this time.**

LETTER OF INTRODUCTION FROM A SCHOOL SUPPORT TEAM COORDINATOR

[Letterhead]

[Date]
[Address]

Dear [Name]:

Thank you for agreeing to serve on the School Support Team for _____ in _____ ISD. The *Entry Visit* is scheduled to be held on _____ at _____ a.m. at _____. Prior to this meeting, there will be an orientation meeting for the School Support Team at _____ a.m. Please be on time, as this will be our only opportunity to visit as a team prior to meeting with the Campus Leadership Team. Enclosed you will find your packet of information, which includes the following:

• **Entry Visit/School Support Teams Agenda:** This agenda was agreed upon by the Campus Leadership Team. *[Authors' note: For a sample, please see fig. 2.4]*

• **Campus Profile:** Please look over this information. It will help you to better understand this campus. You will probably want to pay close attention to the [Texas Assessment of Academic Skills] test information, student population, and prior professional development opportunities. *[See Appendix J.]*

• **School Support Team/Campus Leadership Team Planning Form:** Please bring this form to the first visit. We will use it with the Campus Leadership Team at the end of the day as we assist them in planning and goal setting. *[See fig. 2.2.]*

• **School Support Team Member's Log:** This log will provide valuable information to me as I coordinate this effort. I need to know what has taken place between you and this campus. Thank you, in advance, for your efficiency in keeping up with this log. Please mail or fax it to me in a timely manner after a contact has occurred. *[See fig. 2.3.]*

I believe you will find this to be a valuable experience for your own professional growth. When practitioner and practitioner can sit down together and discuss what is good for kids, only great things can come about. I look forward to working with you and witnessing some dramatic improvement in our schools. Thank you for your time, effort, and commitment to help make our schools even better than they are.

Sincerely,

[Name]
School Support Team Coordinator

CAMPUS PROFILE INFORMATION FORM

_____   _____
(District)   (Campus)

_____   _____
(Campus address)   (Phone number)

_____   _____
(Fax)   (Grade span)

Number of teachers_____   Number of paraprofessionals_____   Number of administrators_____

Number of students enrolled_____

STUDENT POPULATION

_____ % African American   _____ % Migrant

_____ % Hispanic   _____ % Special education

_____ % White (European American)   _____ % LEP

_____ % Native American   _____ % Economically disadvantaged

_____ % Asian   _____ % Gifted/talented

TEACHER POPULATION   LEVEL OF TEACHER EXPERIENCE

_____ % African American   _____ % 0–5 years

_____ % Hispanic   _____ % 6–10 years

_____ % White (European American)   _____ % 11–20 years

_____ % Native American   _____ % more than 20 years

_____ % Asian   _____ % with bachelor's degree

_____ % Minority staff   _____ % with master's degree

_____ % Turnover per year   _____ % with doctorate degree

ACCOUNTABILITY

Accreditation rating_____ Exemplary_____ Recognized_____ Accredited_____ Accredited Warned_____
(please check)

Dropout rate_____%   Attendance_____%   Graduation Rate_____ %

CAMPUS LEADERSHIP TEAM MEMBERS

| (please check) | | | Grade/ | Years of | Have children in school? |
Parent	Teacher	Name	Subject	Experience	In special program?
_____	_____	_____	_____	_____	_____
_____	_____	_____	_____	_____	_____
_____	_____	_____	_____	_____	_____
_____	_____	_____	_____	_____	_____
_____	_____	_____	_____	_____	_____
_____	_____	_____	_____	_____	_____
_____	_____	_____	_____	_____	_____
_____	_____	_____	_____	_____	_____
_____	_____	_____	_____	_____	_____
_____	_____	_____	_____	_____	_____
_____	_____	_____	_____	_____	_____
_____	_____	_____	_____	_____	_____
_____	_____	_____	_____	_____	_____
_____	_____	_____	_____	_____	_____
_____	_____	_____	_____	_____	_____
_____	_____	_____	_____	_____	_____
_____	_____	_____	_____	_____	_____

TAAS SCORES   (PAST THREE YEARS)   PERCENT PASSING
(Texas Assessment of Academic Skills)

Population: All Students

GRADE LEVEL	READING			WRITING			MATH		
	'94	'95	'96	'94	'95	'96	'94	'95	'96
3	___	___	___	___	___	___	___	___	___
4	___	___	___	___	___	___	___	___	___
5	___	___	___	___	___	___	___	___	___
6	___	___	___	___	___	___	___	___	___
7	___	___	___	___	___	___	___	___	___
8	___	___	___	___	___	___	___	___	___
EXIT	___	___	___	___	___	___	___	___	___

Population:

GRADE LEVEL	READING			WRITING			MATH		
	'94	'95	'96	'94	'95	'96	'94	'95	'96
3	___	___	___	___	___	___	___	___	___
4	___	___	___	___	___	___	___	___	___
5	___	___	___	___	___	___	___	___	___
6	___	___	___	___	___	___	___	___	___
7	___	___	___	___	___	___	___	___	___
8	___	___	___	___	___	___	___	___	___
EXIT	___	___	___	___	___	___	___	___	___

TAAS SCORES   (PAST THREE YEARS)   PERCENT PASSING
(Texas Assessment of Academic Skills)

Population: _____

GRADE LEVEL	READING			WRITING			MATH		
	'94	'95	'96	'94	'95	'96	'94	'95	'96
3	___	___	___	___	___	___	___	___	___
4	___	___	___	___	___	___	___	___	___
5	___	___	___	___	___	___	___	___	___
6	___	___	___	___	___	___	___	___	___
7	___	___	___	___	___	___	___	___	___
8	___	___	___	___	___	___	___	___	___
EXIT	___	___	___	___	___	___	___	___	___

Population: _____

GRADE LEVEL	READING			WRITING			MATH		
	'94	'95	'96	'94	'95	'96	'94	'95	'96
3	___	___	___	___	___	___	___	___	___
4	___	___	___	___	___	___	___	___	___
5	___	___	___	___	___	___	___	___	___
6	___	___	___	___	___	___	___	___	___
7	___	___	___	___	___	___	___	___	___
8	___	___	___	___	___	___	___	___	___
EXIT	___	___	___	___	___	___	___	___	___

(Reproduce as needed)

COMMUNITY RESOURCES

(List)

PROFESSIONAL DEVELOPMENT

(List prior professional development that has occurred)

CAMPUS INITIATIVES
(New; in the planning stage)

(List)

SPECIAL PROGRAMS ON CAMPUS
(Special programs already on campus)

(List)

PARENT/COMMUNITY INVOLVEMENT

(List opportunities for involvement and the percentage of attendance)

Campus Plan Identified:

STRENGTHS   PRIORITIES FOR IMPROVEMENT

CAMPUS MISSION STATEMENT:

(Please attach a copy of your campus plan and your campus Academic Excellence Indicator System report.)

PROGRAM DESCRIPTION GUIDE

School Support Teams/Schoolwide Campuses

Check all
that apply

Indicate the positions represented on your school support team:

❑ teacher
❑ pupil service personnel
❑ distinguished educators
❑ representative from institution of higher education
❑ regional educational center personnel
❑ outside consultant groups
❑ other _____
❑ other _____

Indicate the strategies used to work with schoolwide campuses:

❑ assist schools with planning or implementing schoolwide programs
❑ assist schools in the school improvement process and schools in need of improvement
❑ make recommendations as schools develop their schoolwide program plan or school improvement plan
❑ other _____
❑ other _____

During the operation of the schoolwide program or during school improvement activities, a school support team shall

❑ periodically review the progress of the school in enabling children in the school to meet the state's student performance standards
❑ identify problems in the design and operation of the instructional program
❑ make recommendations for improvement to the school and LEA
❑ other _____
❑ other _____

Indicate the steps that have been taken in schoolwide planning:

❑ establish a planning team
❑ determine how the planning team will consistently communicate with the school community
❑ conduct a comprehensive needs assessment
❑ organize data into a school profile
❑ investigate the research base
❑ draft comprehensive goals and specific objectives
❑ complete the final plan
❑ other _____
❑ other _____

OVERHEADS: BRIEF LECTURE ON IMPROVING AMERICA'S SCHOOLS ACT, SECTION 1117

O V E R H E A D 1

Each state agency shall establish a statewide system of *intensive and sustained support* and improvement for schools receiving funding under this act, including schoolwide programs and schools in need of school improvement, in order to increase the opportunity for all students in such schools to meet the state's content standards and student performance standards.

Each school support team shall include *teachers, pupil services personnel, representatives of organizations knowledgeable about successful schoolwide programs or comprehensive school reform* (especially distinguished educators), and *other persons knowledgeable about research and practice on teaching and learning*, particularly about strategies for improving the educational opportunities for low achieving students (including alternative and applied learning), such as representatives of higher education, regional educational laboratories, and outside consultant groups.

A school support team shall *work cooperatively* with each school and *make recommendations* as the school develops its schoolwide program plan or school improvement plan, *review each plan*, and make recommendations to the school and school district.

During the operation of the schoolwide program

or during school improvement activities,

a school support team shall

- Periodically review the progress of the school

  in enabling children in the school

  to meet the state's student performance

  standards;

- Identify problems in the design and operation

  of the instructional program; and

- Make recommendations to the school and

  school district.

If funds are sufficient, school support teams shall provide information and assistance to schools with 75% or more of their students in poverty, schools identified for school improvement, and other schools in need of improvement.

Getting Reform Right: What Works and What Doesn't

There are as many myths as there are truths associated with change, Messrs. Fullan and Miles assert, and educators need to deepen the way they think about change. To that end, the authors analyze seven reasons change fails and offer seven "propositions" for successful change.

BY MICHAEL G. FULLAN AND MATTHEW B. MILES

AFTER YEARS of failed education reform, educators are more and more in the habit of saying that "knowledge of the change process" is crucial. But few people really know what that means. The phrase is used superficially, glibly, as if saying it over and over will lead to understanding and appropriate action.

We do believe that knowing about the change process is crucial. But there are as many myths as there are truths associated with change, and it is time to deepen the way we think about change. We need to assess our knowledge more critically and describe what we know. One needs a good deal of sophistication to grasp the fundamentals of the change process and to use that knowledge wisely.

We also believe that serious education reform will never be achieved until there is a significant increase in the number of people — leaders and other participants alike — who have come to internalize and habitually act on basic knowledge of how successful change takes place. Reformers talk of the need for deeper, second-order changes in the structures and cul-

MICHAEL G. FULLAN is dean of the Faculty of Education at the University of Toronto. MATTHEW B. MILES is a senior research associate with the Center for Policy Research, New York, N.Y.

tures of schools, rather than superficial first-order changes.[1] But no change would be more fundamental than a dramatic expansion of the capacity of individuals and organizations to understand and deal with change. This generic capacity is worth more than a hundred individual success stories of implementing specific innovations. As we shall see, even individual success stories don't last long without an appreciation of how to keep changes alive.

Rather than develop a new strategy for each new wave of reform, we must use basic knowledge about the do's and don'ts of bringing about *continuous improvement*. In this article we present this knowledge in the form of seven basic reasons why reform fails — and seven propositions that could lead to success.

WHY REFORM FAILS

Schools and districts are overloaded with problems — and, ironically, with solutions that don't work. Thus things get worse instead of better. Even our rare success stories appear as isolated pockets of excellence and are as likely to atrophy as to prosper over time. We get glimpses of the power of change, but we have little confidence that we know how to harness forces for continuous improvement. The problem is not really lack of

innovation, but the enormous overload of fragmented, uncoordinated, and ephemeral attempts at change.

We begin with reasons why typical approaches do not work. In our view there are seven basic reasons why reforms fail. Though each one has its own form, these seven should be understood in combination, as a set.

1. Faulty maps of change. It's hard to get to a destination when your map doesn't accurately represent the territory you're to traverse. Everyone involved in school reform — teachers, administrators, parents, students, district staff members, consultants, board members, state department officials, legislators, materials developers, publishers, test-makers, teacher educators, researchers — has a personal map of how change proceeds. These constructs are often expressed in the form of a proposition or statement.

1. Resistance is inevitable, because people resist change.

2. Every school is unique.

3. *Plus ça change, plus c'est la même chose.*

4. Schools are essentially conservative institutions, harder to change than other organizations.

5. You just have to live reform one day at a time.

6. You need a mission, objectives, and a series of tasks laid out well in advance.

Source: Phi Delta Kappan. (June 1992). Reprinted with the permission of Phi Delta Kappan.

7. You can never please everyone, so just push ahead with reforms.

8. Full participation of everyone involved in a change is essential.

9. Keep it simple, stupid: go for small, easy changes rather than big, demanding ones.

10. Mandate change, because people won't do it otherwise.

People act on their maps. But maps such as these don't provide reliable or valid guidance. Some, like number 1, are simply self-sealing and tautological. Others, like number 2, are true in the abstract but totally unhelpful in providing guidance. Imagine if a Michelin guide book were to tell you that "each restaurant is unique," refuse to make ratings, and tell you that you're on your own.

Some, like number 3, have the seductive appearance of truth, though they are mostly false. It stretches the bounds of credulity to say that the schools we see today are no different from those of yesteryear or that all change efforts are self-defeating. Such maps are self-defeating. At their worst, they tell us that nothing really changes — and that nothing will work. On such self-exculpatory propositions as number 4, there's simply very little evidence, and what there is leads to the verdict of "not proven."[2]

Sometimes our maps are in conflict with themselves or with the maps of colleagues. For example, number 5 advocates the virtues of improvisation, while number 6 lauds rational planning. In fact, the literature on organizational change and a recent study of major change in urban high schools show that *neither* statement is valid as a guide to successful school reform.[3] The same appears to be true for propositions 7 and 8.

Still other mapping statements are directly contradicted by empirical evidence. For example, though number 9 looks obvious, studies of change have repeatedly found that substantial change efforts that address multiple problems are more likely to succeed and survive than small-scale, easily trivialized innovations.[4]

And number 10, as attractive as it may be politically, simply doesn't work. Indeed, it often makes matters worse. You can't mandate important changes, because they require skill, motivation, commitment, and discretionary judgment on the part of those who must change.[5]

Our aim here is not to debunk all our maps. Maps are crucial. But unless a map is a valid representation of the territory, we won't get where we want to go. Later in this article, we will outline a map that,

We must have an approach to reform that acknowledges that we may not know all the answers.

we believe, corresponds well with the real territory of change.

2. Complex problems. Another major reason for the failure of reform is that the solutions are not easy — or even known in many cases. A number of years ago Arthur Wise labeled this problem the "hyperrationalization" of reform:

> To create goals for education is to will that something occur. But goals, in the absence of a theory of how to achieve them, are mere wishful thinking. If there is no reason to believe a goal is attainable — perhaps evidenced by the fact that it has never been attained — then a rational planning model may not result in goal attainment.[6]

The reform agenda has broadened in fundamental ways in the last five years. One need only mention the comprehensive reform legislation adopted in virtually every state and the scores of restructuring efforts in order to realize that current change efforts are enormously complex — both in the substance of their goals and in the capacity of individuals and institutions to carry out and coordinate reforms.

Education *is* a complex system, and its reform is even more complex. Even if one considers only seemingly simple, first-order changes, the number of components and their interrelationships are

staggering: curriculum and instruction, school organization, student services, community involvement, teacher inservice training, assessment, reporting, and evaluation. Deeper, second-order changes in school cultures, teacher/student relationships, and values and expectations of the system are all the more daunting.

Furthermore, higher-order educational goals for all students require knowledge and abilities that we have never demonstrated. In many cases, we simply don't know how to proceed; solutions have yet to be developed. This is no reason to stop trying, but we must remember that it is folly to act as if we know how to solve complex problems in short order. We must have an approach to reform that acknowledges that we don't necessarily know all the answers, that is conducive to developing solutions as we go along, and that sustains our commitment and persistence to stay with the problem until we get somewhere. In other words, we need a different map for solving complex rather than simple problems.

3. Symbols over substance. In the RAND-sponsored study of federal programs supporting educational change, Paul Berman and Milbrey McLaughlin found that some school districts adopted external innovations for opportunistic reasons rather than to solve a particular problem. These apparent reforms brought extra resources (which were not necessarily used for the intended purpose), symbolized that action was being taken (whether or not follow-up occurred), and furthered the careers of the innovators (whether or not the innovation succeeded). Thus the mere appearance of innovation is sometimes sufficient for achieving political success.

Education reform is as much a political as an educational process, and it has both negative and positive aspects. One need not question the motives of political decision makers to appreciate the negative. Political time lines are at variance with the time lines for education reform. This difference often results in vague goals, unrealistic schedules, a preoccupation with symbols of reform (new legislation, task forces, commissions, and the like), and shifting priorities as political pressures ebb and flow.

We acknowledge that symbols are essential for success. They serve to crystallize images and to attract and generate political power and financial resources. Symbols can also provide personal and collective meaning and give people faith and confidence when they are dealing with unclear goals and complex situations.[7] They are essential for galvanizing visions, acquiring resources, and carrying out concerted action. When symbols and substance are congruent, they form a powerful combination.

Nonetheless, reform often fails because politics favors symbols over substance. Substantial change in practice requires a lot of hard and clever work "on the ground," which is not the strong point of political players. After several experiences with the dominance of symbolic change over substantive change, people become cynical and take the next change that comes along much less seriously.

Symbolic change does not have to be without substance, however. Indeed, the best examples of effective symbols are grounded in rituals, ceremonies, and other events in the daily life of an organization. While we cannot have effective reform without symbols, we can easily have symbols without effective reform —

> # Reforms also fail because our attempts to solve problems are frequently superficial.

the predominant experience of most educators and one that predisposes them to be skeptical about *all* reforms.

4. Impatient and superficial solutions. Reforms also fail because our attempts to solve problems are frequently superficial. Superficial solutions, introduced quickly in an atmosphere of crisis, normally make matters worse.[8] This problem is all the more serious now that

we are tackling large-scale reforms, for the consequences of failure are much more serious.

Reforms in structure are especially susceptible to superficiality and unrealistic time lines, because they can be launched through political or administrative mandates. Two examples at opposite ends of the political spectrum provide cases in point. A recent study of the impact of statewide testing in two states found that, while new testing mandates caused action at the local level, they also narrowed the curriculum and created adverse conditions for reform:

> [C]oping with the pressure to attain satisfactory results in high-stakes tests caused educators to develop almost a "crisis mentality" in their approach, in that they jumped quickly into "solutions" to address a specific issue. They narrowed the range of instructional strategies from which they selected means to instruct their students; they narrowed the content of the material they chose to present to students; and they narrowed the range of course offerings available to students.[9]

Site-based management — opposite in many ways to the strategy of centralized testing — also shows problems associated with structural reforms. Daniel Levine and Eugene Eubanks, among others, have indicated how school-based models often result in changes in formal decision-making structures but rarely result in a focus on developing instructional skills or on changing the culture of schools.[10] There are numerous other examples of new legislation and policies — career ladders, mentoring and induction policies, testing and competency requirements, and so on — being rushed into place with little forethought about possible negative consequences and side effects.

A related bane of reform is faddism. Schools, districts, and states are under tremendous pressure to reform. Innovation and reform are big business, politically and economically. The temptation is great to latch on to the quick fix, to go along with the trend, to react uncritically to endorsed innovations as they come and go. Local educators experience most school reforms as fads.

There are two underlying problems. One is that mistaken or superficial solutions are introduced; the other is that,

> # Reform often fails because politics favors symbols over substance. Substantial change in practice requires a lot of hard, clever work "on the ground," which is not the strong point of political players. After several experiences with the dominance of symbolic change over substantive change, people become cynical.

even when the solution is on the right track, hasty implementation leads to failure. Structural solutions are relatively easy to initiate under the right political conditions, but they are no substitute for the hard work, skill, and commitment needed to blend different structural changes into a successful reform effort. In other words, changes in structure must go hand in hand with changes in culture and in the individual and collective capacity to work through new structures. Because education reform is so complex, we cannot know in advance exactly which new structures and behavioral patterns should go together or how they should mesh. But we do know that neglecting one or the other is a surefire recipe for failure.

5. **Misunderstanding resistance.** Things hardly ever go easily during change efforts. Since change necessarily involves people, and people can commit willed actions, it seems natural to attribute progress that is slower than we might wish to their "resistance." Before a recent workshop, one of us asked a group of principals to list the problems they faced in a specific change project. More than half said "resistance" — variously known as intransigence, entrenchment, fearfulness, reluctance to buy in, complacency, unwillingness to alter behaviors, and failure to recognize the need for change. These traits were attributed to teachers and other staff members, though not to the principals themselves.

But it is usually unproductive to label an attitude or action "resistance." It diverts attention from real problems of implementation, such as diffuse objectives, lack of technical skill, or insufficient resources for change. In effect, the label also individualizes issues of change and converts everything into a matter of "attitude." Because such labeling places the blame (and the responsibility for the solution) on others, it immobilizes people and leads to "if only" thinking.

Change does involve individual attitudes and behaviors, but they need to be framed as natural responses to transition, not misunderstood as "resistance." During transitions from a familiar to a new state of affairs, individuals must normally confront the loss of the old and commit themselves to the new, unlearn old beliefs and behaviors and learn new ones, and move from anxiousness and uncer-

tainty to stabilization and coherence. Any significant change involves a period of intense personal and organizational learning and problem solving. People need supports for such work, not displays of impatience.

Failure to institutionalize an innovation underlies the disappearance of many reforms.

Blaming "resistance" for the slow pace of reform also keeps us from understanding that individuals and groups faced with something new need to assess the change for its genuine possibilities and for how it bears on their self-interest. From computers across the curriculum, to mainstreaming, to portfolio assessments, to a radical change in the time schedule, significant changes normally require extra effort during the transitional stage. Moreover, there's little certainty about the kinds of outcomes that may ensue for students and teachers (and less assurance that they will be any better than the status quo). These are legitimate issues that deserve careful attention.

Many reform initiatives are ill-conceived, and many others are fads. The most authentic response to such efforts is resistance. Nevertheless, when resistance is misunderstood, we are immediately set on a self-defeating path. Reframing the legitimate basis of most forms of resistance will allow us to get a more productive start and to isolate the real problems of improvement.

6. **Attrition of pockets of success.** There are many examples of successful reforms in individual schools — cases in which the strong efforts of teachers, principals, and district administrators have brought about significant changes in

classroom and school practice.[11] We do not have much evidence about the durability of such successes, but we have reason to believe that they may not survive if the conditions under which they developed are changed.

Successful reforms have typically required enormous effort on the part of one or more individuals — effort that may not be sustainable over time. For example, staff collaboration takes much energy and time to develop, yet it can disappear overnight when a few key people leave. What happens outside the school — such as changes in district policies on the selection and transfer of teachers and principals — can easily undo gains that have been made.

Local innovators, even when they are successful in the short run, may burn themselves out or unwittingly seal themselves off from the surrounding environment. Thus schools can become hotbeds of innovation and reform in the absence of external support, but they cannot *stay* innovative without the continuing support of the district and other agencies. Innovative schools may enjoy external support from a critically important sponsor (e.g., the district superintendent) or from a given agency only to see that support disappear when the sponsor moves on or the agency changes policies. Of course, the failure to institutionalize an innovation and build it into the normal structures and practices of the organization underlies the disappearance of many reforms.[12]

We suspect that few things are more discouraging than working hard against long odds over a period of time to achieve a modicum of success — only to see it evaporate in short order as unrelated events take their toll. It is not enough to achieve isolated pockets of success. Reform fails unless we can demonstrate that pockets of success add up to new structures, procedures, and school cultures that press for continuous improvement. So far there is little such evidence.

7. **Misuse of knowledge about the change process.** The final problem is related to a particular version of faulty maps: "knowledge" of the change process is often cited as the authority for taking certain actions. Statements such as "Ownership is the key to reform," "Lots of inservice training is required," "The school is the unit of change," "Vision and leadership are critical," and so on are all

half-truths. Taken literally, they can be misused.

Reform is systemic, and actions based on knowledge of the change process must be systemic, too. To succeed we need to link a number of key aspects of knowledge and maintain the connections before and during the process of change. In the following section we offer seven such themes, which we believe warrant being called propositions for success.

PROPOSITIONS FOR SUCCESS

The seven basic themes or lessons derived from current knowledge of successful change form a set and must be contemplated in relation to one another. When it comes to reform, partial theories are not very useful. We can say flatly that reform will not be achieved until these seven orientations have been incorporated into the thinking and reflected in the actions of those involved in change efforts.

1. Change is learning — loaded with uncertainty. Change is a process of coming to grips with new personal meaning, and so it is a learning process. Peter Marris states the problem this way:

> When those who have the power to manipulate changes act as if they have only to explain, and when their explanations are not at once accepted, shrug off opposition as ignorance or prejudice, they express a profound contempt for the meaning of lives other than their own. For the reformers have already assimilated these changes to their purposes, and worked out a reformulation which makes sense to them, perhaps through months or years of analysis and debate. If they deny others the chance to do the same, they treat them as puppets dangling by the threads of their own conceptions.[13]

Even well-developed innovations represent new meaning and new learning for those who encounter them initially and require time to assimilate them. So many studies have documented this early period of difficulty that we have given it a label — "the implementation dip."[14] Even in cases where reform eventually succeeds, things will often go wrong before they go right. Michael Huberman and Matthew Miles found that the absence of early difficulty in a reform ef-

fort was usually a sign that not much was being attempted; superficial or trivial change was being substituted for substantial change.[15]

More complex reforms, such as restructuring, represent even greater uncertainty: first, because more is being attempted; second, because the solution is not known in advance. In short, anxiety, difficulties, and uncertainty are *intrinsic to all successful change*.

Ownership of a reform cannot be achieved *in advance of* learning something new.

One can see why a climate that encourages risk-taking is so critical. People will not venture into uncertainty unless there is an appreciation that difficulties encountered are a natural part of the process. And if people do not venture into uncertainty, no significant change will occur.

Understanding successful change as learning also puts ownership in perspective. In our view, ownership of a reform cannot be achieved *in advance* of learning something new. A deep sense of ownership comes only through learning. In this sense, ownership is stronger in the middle of a successful change process than at the beginning and stronger still at the end. Ownership is both a process and a state.

The first proposition for success, then, is to understand that all change involves learning and that all learning involves coming to understand and to be good at something new. Thus conditions that support learning must be part and parcel of any change effort. Such conditions are also necessary for the valid rejection of particular changes, because many people reject complex innovations prematurely,

that is, before they are in a sound position to make such a judgment.

2. Change is a journey, not a blueprint. If change involved implementing single, well-developed, proven innovations one at a time, perhaps we could make blueprints for change. But school districts and schools are in the business of implementing a bewildering array of innovations and policies simultaneously. Moreover, reforms that aim at restructuring are so multifaceted and complex that solutions for any particular setting cannot be known in advance. If one tries to account for the complexity of the situation with an equally complex implementation plan, the process will become unwieldy, cumbersome, and usually unsuccessful.

There can be no blueprints for change, because rational planning models for complex social change (such as education reform) do not work. Rather, what is needed is a guided journey. Karen Seashore Louis and Matthew Miles provide a clear analysis of this evolutionary planning process in their study of urban high schools involved in major change efforts:

> The evolutionary perspective rests on the assumption that the environment both inside and outside organizations is often chaotic. No specific plan can last for very long, because it will either become outmoded due to changing external pressures, or because disagreement over priorities arises within the organization. Yet there is no reason to assume that the best response is to plan passively, relying on incremental decisions. Instead, the organization can cycle back and forth between efforts to gain normative consensus about what it may become, to plan strategies for getting there, and to carry out decentralized incremental experimentation that harnesses the creativity of all members to the change effort. . . . Strategy is viewed as a flexible tool, rather than a semi-permanent expansion of the mission.[16]

The message is not the traditional "Plan, then do," but "Do, then plan . . . and do and plan some more." Even the development of a shared vision that is central to reform is better thought of as a journey in which people's sense of purpose is identified, considered, and continuously shaped and reshaped.

3. Problems are our friends. School

improvement is a problem-rich process. Change threatens existing interests and routines, heightens uncertainty, and increases complexity. The typical principal in the study of urban schools conducted by Louis and Miles mentioned three or four major problems (and several minor ones) with reform efforts. They ranged from poor coordination to staff polarization and from lack of needed skills to heart attacks suffered by key figures. Problems arise naturally from the demands of the change process itself, from the people involved, and from the structure and procedures of schools and districts. Some are easily solved; others are almost intractable.

It seems perverse to say that problems are our friends, but we cannot develop effective responses to complex situations unless we actively seek and confront real problems that are difficult to solve. Problems are our friends because only through immersing ourselves in problems can we come up with creative solutions. Problems are the route to deeper change and deeper satisfaction. In this sense, effective organizations "embrace problems" rather than avoid them.

Too often, change-related problems are ignored, denied, or treated as an occasion for blame and defense. Success in school reform efforts is much more likely when problems are treated as natural, expected phenomena. Only by tracking problems can we understand what we need to do next to get what we want. Problems must be taken seriously, not attributed to "resistance" or to the ignorance and wrongheadedness of others.

What to do about problems? In their study of urban schools, Louis and Miles classified coping styles, ranging from relatively shallow ones (doing nothing at all, procrastinating, "doing it the usual way," easing off, or increasing pressure) to deeper ones (building personal capacity through training, enhancing system capacity, comprehensive restaffing, or system restructuring/redesign). They found that schools that were least successful at change *always* used shallow coping styles. Schools that were successful in changing could and did make structural changes in an effort to solve difficult problems. However, they were also willing to use Band-Aid solutions when a problem was judged to be minor. It's important to note that successful schools

did *not* have fewer problems than other schools — they just coped with them better.

The enemies of good coping are pas-

Success in school reform efforts is much more likely when problems are treated as natural.

---

sivity, denial, avoidance, conventionality, and fear of being "too radical." Good coping is active, assertive, inventive. It goes to the root of the problem when that is needed.

We cannot cope better through being exhorted to do so. "Deep coping" — the key to solving difficult problems of reform — appears to be more likely when schools are working on a clear, shared vision of where they are heading and when they create an active coping structure (e.g., a coordinating committee or a steering group) that steadily and actively tracks problems and monitors the results of coping efforts. Such a structure benefits from empowerment, brings more resources to bear on problems, and keeps the energy for change focused. In short, the assertive pursuit of problems in the service of continuous improvement is the kind of accountability that can make a difference.

4. Change is resource-hungry. Even a moderate-sized school may spend a million dollars a year on salaries, maintenance, and materials. And that's just for keeping schools as they are, not for changing them. Change demands additional resources for training, for substitutes, for new materials, for new space, and, above all, for time. Change is "resource-hungry" because of what it represents — developing solutions to complex problems, learning new skills, arriving at new insights, all carried out in a so-

cial setting already overloaded with demands. Such serious personal and collective development necessarily demands resources.

Every analysis of the problems of change efforts that we have seen in the last decade of research and practice has concluded that time is the salient issue. Most recently, the survey of urban high schools by Louis and Miles found that the average principal with a schoolwide reform project spent 70 days a year on change management. That's 32% of an administrator's year. The teachers most closely engaged with the change effort spent some 23 days a year, or 13% of their time on reform. Since we have to keep school while we change school, such overloads are to be expected.

But time is energy. And success is likely only when the extra energy requirements of change are met through the provision of released time or through a redesigned schedule that includes space for the extra work of change.

Time is also money. And Louis and Miles discovered that serious change in big-city high schools requires an annual investment of between $50,000 and $100,000. They also found some schools spending five times that much with little to show for it. The key seemed to be whether the money simply went for new jobs and expensive equipment or was spent for local capacity-building (acquiring external assistance, training trainers, leveraging other add-on funds, and so on). Nevertheless, some minimum level of funding is always needed.

Assistance itself can be a major resource for change. It may include training, consulting, coaching, coordination, and capacity-building. Many studies have suggested that good assistance to schools is strong, sustained over years, closely responsive to local needs, and focused on building local capacity. Louis and Miles found that at least 30 days a year of *external* assistance — with more than that provided internally — was essential for success.

We can also think of educational "content resources" — such big ideas as effective schools, teaching for understanding, empowerment, and school-based management — that guide and energize the work of change. In addition, there are psychosocial resources, such as support, commitment, influence, and power. They're supposedly intangible, but they are critical for success.

The work of change requires attention not just to resources, but to "resourcing." The actions required are those of scanning the school and its environment for resources and matching them to existing needs; acquiring resources (buying, negotiating, or just plain grabbing); reworking them for a better fit to the situation; creating time through schedule changes and other arrangements; and building local capacity through the development of such structures as steering groups, coordinating committees, and cadres of local trainers.

Good resourcing requires facing up to the need for funds and abjuring any false pride about self-sufficiency. Above all, it takes willingness to invent, to go outside the frame in garnering and reworking resources. (We are reminded of the principal who used money for the heating system to pay for desperately needed repainting and renovation, saying, "I knew that, if the boiler broke, they'd have to fix it anyway.") The stance is one of steady and tenacious searching for and judicious use of the extra resources that any change requires. Asking for assistance and seeking other resources are signs of strength, not weakness.

5. Change requires the power to manage it. Change initiatives do not run themselves. They require that substantial effort be devoted to such tasks as monitoring implementation, keeping everyone informed of what's happening, linking multiple change projects (typical in most schools), locating unsolved problems, and taking clear coping action. In Louis and Miles' study, such efforts occurred literally 10 times more frequently in successfully changing schools than in unchanging ones.

There appear to be several essential ingredients in the successful management of change. First, the management of change goes best when it is carried out by a *cross-role group* (say, teachers, department heads, administrators, and — often — students and parents). In such a group different worlds collide, more learning occurs, and change is realistically managed. There is much evidence that steering a change effort in this way results in substantially increased teacher commitment.

Second, such a cross-role group needs

legitimacy — i.e., a clear license to steer. It needs an explicit contract, widely understood in the school, as to what kinds of decisions it can make and what money it can spend. Such legitimacy is partly conferred at the front end and partly

---

The management of change goes best when it is carried out by a *cross-role group.*

---

earned through the hard work of decision making and action. Most such groups do encounter staff polarization; they may be seen by others as an unfairly privileged elite; or they may be opposed on ideological grounds. Such polarization — often a sign that empowerment of a steering group is working — can be dealt with through open access to meetings, rotation of membership, and scrupulous reporting.

Third, even empowerment has its problems, and cooperation is required to solve them. Everyone has to learn to take the initiative instead of complaining, to trust colleagues, to live with ambiguity, to face the fact that shared decisions mean conflict. Principals have to rise above the fear of losing control, and they have to hone new skills: initiating actions firmly without being seen as "controlling," supporting others without taking over for them. All these stances and skills are learnable, but they take time. Kenneth Benne remarked 40 years ago that the skills of cooperative work should be "part of the general education of our people."[17] They haven't been, so far. But the technology for teaching these skills exists. It is up to steering groups to learn to work well together, using whatever assistance is required.

Fourth, the power to manage change

does not stop at the schoolhouse door. Successful change efforts are most likely when the local district office is closely engaged with the changing school in a collaborative, supportive way and places few bureaucratic restrictions in the path of reform.

The bottom line is that the development of second-order changes in the culture of schools and in the capacity of teachers, principals, and communities to make a difference *requires* the power to manage the change at the local school level. We do not advocate handing over all decisions to the school. Schools and their environments must have an interactive and negotiated relationship. But complex problems cannot be solved from a distance; the steady growth of the power to manage change must be part of the solution.

6. Change is systemic. Political pressures combine with the segmented, uncoordinated nature of educational organizations to produce a "project mentality."[18] A steady stream of episodic innovations — cooperative learning, effective schools research, classroom management, assessment schemes, career ladders, peer coaching, etc., etc. — come and go. Not only do they fail to leave much of a trace, but they also leave teachers and the public with a growing cynicism that innovation is marginal and politically motivated.

What does it mean to work systemically? There are two aspects: 1) reform must focus on the development and interrelationships of all the main *components* of the system simultaneously — curriculum, teaching and teacher development, community, student support systems, and so on; and 2) reform must focus not just on structure, policy, and regulations but on deeper issues of the *culture* of the system. Fulfilling both requirements is a tall order. But it is possible.

This duality of reform (the need to deal with system components and system culture) must be attended to at both the state and district/school levels. It involves both restructuring and "reculturing."[19] Marshall Smith and Jennifer O'Day have mapped out a comprehensive plan for systemic reform at the state level that illustrates the kind of thinking and strategies involved.[20] At the school/district level, we see in the Toronto region's Learning Consortium a rather clear example of systemic reform

Wishful thinking and legislation have poor records as tools for social betterment.

in action.[21] Schools, supported by their districts, avoid ad hoc innovations and focus on a variety of coordinated short-term and mid- to long-term strategies. The short-term activities include inservice professional development on selected and interrelated themes; mid- to long-term strategies include vision building, initial teacher preparation, selection and induction, promotion procedures and criteria, school-based planning in a system context, curriculum reorganization, and the development of assessments. There is an explicit emphasis on new cultural norms for collaborative work and on the pursuit of continuous improvement.

Systemic reform is complex. Practically speaking, traditional approaches to innovation and reform in education have not been successful in bringing about lasting improvement. Systemic reform looks to be both more efficient and more effective, even though this proposition is less proven empirically than our other six. However, both conceptually and practically, it does seem to be on the right track.[22]

7. All large-scale change is implemented locally. Change cannot be accomplished from afar. This cardinal rule crystallizes the previous six propositions. The ideas that change is learning, change is a journey, problems are our friends, change is resource-hungry, change requires the power to manage, and change is systemic all embody the fact that *local* implementation by everyday teachers, principals, parents, and students is the only way that change happens.

This observation has both an obvious and a less obvious meaning. The former reminds us all that any interest in system-wide reform must be accompanied by a preoccupation with how it plays itself out locally. The less obvious implication can be stated as a caution: we should not assume that only the local level counts and hand everything over to the individual school. A careful reading of the seven propositions together shows that extra-local agencies have critical — though decidedly not traditional — roles to play. Most fundamentally, their role is to help bring the seven propositions to life at the local level.

Modern societies are facing terrible problems, and education reform is seen as a major source of hope for solving them. But wishful thinking and legislation have deservedly poor track records as tools for social betterment. As educators increasingly acknowledge that the "change process is crucial," they ought to know what that means at the level at which change actually takes place. Whether we are on the receiving or initiating end of change (as all of us are at one time or another), we need to understand why education reform frequently fails, and we need to internalize and live out valid propositions for its success. Living out the seven propositions for successful change means not only making the change process more explicit within our own minds and actions, but also contributing to the knowledge of change on the part of those with whom we interact. Being knowledgeable about the change process may be both the best defense and the best offense we have in achieving substantial education reform.

1. Larry Cuban, "Reforming, Again, Again, and Again," *Educational Researcher*, April 1990, pp. 3-13; Richard F. Elmore, ed., *Restructuring Schools* (San Francisco: Jossey-Bass, 1990); and Michael Fullan, with Suzanne Steigelbauer, *The New Meaning of Educational Change* (New York: Teachers College Press, 1991).

2. Matthew B. Miles, "Mapping the Common Properties of Schools," in Rolf Lehming and Michael Kane, eds., *Improving Schools: Using What We Know* (Santa Monica, Calif.: Sage, 1981), pp. 42-114; and Matthew B. Miles and Karen Seashore Louis, "Research on Institutionalization: A Reflective Review," in Matthew B. Miles, Mats Ekholm, and Rolf Vandenberghe, eds., *Lasting School Improvement: Exploring the Process of Institutionalization* (Leuven, Belgium: Acco, 1987), pp. 24-44.

3. Karen Seashore Louis and Matthew B. Miles, *Improving the Urban High School: What Works and Why* (New York: Teachers College Press, 1990).

4. Paul Berman and Milbrey W. McLaughlin, *Federal Programs Supporting Educational Change, Vol. VIII: Implementing and Sustaining Innovations* (Santa Monica, Calif.: RAND Corporation, 1977); and Michael Huberman and Matthew B. Miles, *Innovation Up Close: How School Improvement Works* (New York: Plenum, 1984).

5. Milbrey W. McLaughlin, "The Rand Change Agent Study Revisited: Macro Perspectives and Micro Realities," *Educational Researcher*, December 1990, pp. 11-16.

6. Arthur Wise, "Why Educational Policies Often Fail: The Hyperrationalization Hypothesis," *Curriculum Studies*, vol. 1, 1977, p. 48.

7. Lee Bolman and Terrence Deal, *Reframing Organizations* (San Francisco: Jossey-Bass, 1990).

8. Samuel D. Sieber, *Fatal Solutions* (Norwood, N.J.: Ablex, 1982).

9. H. Dickson Corbett and Bruce Wilson, *Testing, Reform, and Rebellion* (Norwood, N.J.: Ablex, 1990), p. 207.

10. Daniel U. Levine and Eugene E. Eubanks, "Site-Based Management: Engine for Reform or Pipedream? Pitfalls and Prerequisites for Success in Site-Based Management," unpublished manuscript, University of Missouri, Kansas City.

11. Bruce Joyce et al., "School Renewal as Cultural Change," *Educational Leadership*, November 1989, pp. 70-77; Louis and Miles, op. cit.; and Richard Wallace, Paul LeMahieu, and William Bickel, "The Pittsburgh Experience: Achieving Commitment to Comprehensive Staff Development," in Bruce Joyce, ed., *Changing School Culture Through Staff Development* (Alexandria, Va.: Association for Supervision and Curriculum Development, 1990), pp. 185-202.

12. Miles and Louis, op. cit.; and Matthew B. Miles and Mats Ekholm, "Will New Structures *Stay* Restructured?," paper presented at the annual meeting of the American Educational Research Association, Chicago, 1991.

13. Peter Marris, *Loss and Change* (New York: Doubleday, 1975), p. 166.

14. Fullan, with Steigelbauer, op. cit.

15. Huberman and Miles, op. cit.

16. Louis and Miles, p. 193.

17. Kenneth D. Benne, "Theory of Cooperative Planning," *Teachers College Record*, vol. 53, 1952, pp. 429-35.

18. Marshall Smith and Jennifer O'Day, "Systemic School Reform," in Susan Fuhrman and Bruce Malen, eds., *The Politics of Curriculum and Testing* (Philadelphia: Falmer Press, 1990), pp. 233-67.

19. "Systemic reform" is both a more accurate and a more powerful label than "restructuring" because it explicitly encompasses both structure and culture. See Andy Hargreaves, "Restructuring Restructuring: Postmodernity and the Prospects for Educational Change," paper presented at the annual meeting of the American Educational Research Association, Chicago, 1991.

20. Smith and O'Day, op. cit.

21. Nancy Watson and Michael Fullan, "Beyond School District-University Partnerships," in Michael Fullan and Andy Hargreaves, eds., *Teacher Development and Change* (Toronto: Falmer Press, 1992), pp. 213-42.

22. See Peter Senge, *The Fifth Discipline* (New York: Doubleday, 1990); and Michael G. Fullan, *Productive Educational Change: Going Deeper* (London: Falmer Press, forthcoming). **K**

RECOMMENDATIONS FROM THE TEXAS SCHOOL SUPPORT TEAM PILOT INITIATIVE

Recommendations for SST planning and implementation can be collapsed into four categories: creating entree, building relationships, facilitating meaningful planning, and enhancing commitment. Recommendations highlight effective practices of the SST process.

Recommendations for Creating Entree:

1. Ensure the support of the principal prior to the SST visit.

2. Include as many district and school constituencies in the initial visit to clarify the purposes of the SST process and collaboratively identify strengths and needs. District and school constituencies include the superintendent, principal, central office director of federal programs, teachers, paraprofessionals, student services personnel, parents, community members, and students.

3. Propose an agenda in advance of the visit that includes a school site tour and opportunities for the school site to specify the kinds of expertise they would most appreciate from SST members.

4. Agree on a tentative time line for site visits, and encourage adequate time for school site participants to plan, implement, evaluate, and revise new ideas for change.

Recommendations for Building Relationships:

1. Ensure that all SST members have an opportunity to introduce themselves, their professional backgrounds, the forms of support they are able to offer, and ways in which school site participants might easily access support.

2. Ensure that school site participants have an opportunity to introduce themselves, their professional backgrounds, and the forms of support they are able to offer.

3. Propose clear and purposeful agendas that complement a school's strengths and provide maximum input from school site participants.

4. Allow opportunities for informal interaction, including personalized school site tours.

5. Engage in processes that reinforce the school site as the locus of actions and decision making.

6. Actively share resources at and between visits and follow through with personal commitments in a timely manner.

7. Whenever possible, participate in school processes and functions that are not directly related to the SST process. For example, attend a staff meeting, an awards ceremony, and other significant events.

8. Actively communicate empathy for the complexity of developing solutions to substantive challenges within a demanding social and professional setting.

9. Clearly identify short-term and long-range success, and articulate success openly for the morale of the school as well as the benefit of other sites that are in search of new ideas.

Recommendations for Facilitating Meaningful Planning:

1. Arrange for SST members to meet and collaborate on roles and responsibilities.

2. Support school sites in the development of their school site improvement teams and decision-making processes.

3. Maintain a focus on the entire school program and its influence on student achievement.

4. Facilitate and collaborate with school sites on processes such as reflective practice and collabo-

rative inquiry that build on prior knowledge, maximize the personal and professional relevance of school change, and encourage thoughtful experimentation.

5. Assist school sites in understanding the evolutionary nature of planning processes and the need for flexibility in as much as there are no blueprints or enduring "rational" models for change. As the Texas Education Agency has articulated, "one size does not fit all."

6. Locate and share resources generously for teachers' personal and collective development.

7. Facilitate an ongoing examination of the change process, including the positive attributes of uncertainty and conflict and different working styles.

8. Encourage cross-role groups of, for example, teachers, administrators, department heads, parents, and students for a broad range of perspectives on issues and opportunities, shared responsibility for success, and expansive communication throughout the school community.

Recommendations for Enhancing Commitment:

1. Prior to the conclusion of all meetings, engage school site participants in developing a clear plan of action, identifying useful resources, coordinating meeting times, and selecting individual as well as collective responsibilities for implementing short-term and long-range goals.

2. Establish procedures for accessing interim assistance from SST members (e.g., phone assistance or e-mail addresses)

3. Engage the group in establishing the purpose of and setting the agenda for the next visit.

4. Ensure the support of the principal and, if possible, the superintendent.

5. Prior to the conclusion of all meetings encourage reflective processes for "checking in" on thoughts and feelings related to the group's progress toward a vision of improved student performance. Additionally, encourage feedback on the SST process and encourage suggestions for making the process more effective.

6. At all meetings, invite school site participants to discuss school and classroom initiatives and highlights that have occurred subsequent to the last meeting, and to problem solve emerging challenges.

7. Follow through, as SST members, on all commitments.

SCHOOL REFORM STUDY GROUP DIALOGUE GUIDE

The following pages (105–121) have been selected to encourage reflection on issues influencing school reform and to stimulate a discussion of what schools and school districts can do to support the success of reform initiatives.

Before you begin, please select a group facilitator, a notetaker, and a reporter who will record the large group's dialogue.

1. Briefly familiarize yourselves with the materials.

2. Focus on Item 2, pp. 105–117, "Promising Practices That Foster Inclusive Education" by Alice Udvari-Solner and Jacqueline S. Thousand (from *Creating an Inclusive School* [1995], pp. 87–109, edited by Richard A. Villa and Jacqueline S. Thousand, Alexandria, Va.: Association for Supervision and Curriculum Development). It is written from a special education perspective, but it has strong implications for *all* students. Please review it with the understanding that "what is good for the few is good for the many."

3. Each member of the group selects one or two sections to read and synthesize for the entire group.

    a. Identify three key points to share with the entire group.

    b. Discuss the implications of the key points for schoolwide planning.

    c. Recommend a possible "next step" with respect to further examining the selected topic.

4. If you have time and are able to direct your attention, as a group, to another resource, clarify your goal in reviewing the resource and ask each group member to identify two or three considerations and/or recommendations for schools in your community. For example, if you review Creating a Restructuring Agreement *[Authors' note: Please see fig. 3.12, p. 52]*, your goal might be to determine how a restructuring agreement might support a schoolwide planning process. Next you might want to (a) consider elements of the agreement that you find particularly relevant, and (b) suggest recommendations for working with a school to create a restructuring agreement that is customized to the school's needs.

5. Another resource your Study Group may wish to examine is the article entitled "Building Capacity Through School Support Teams" (Item 3, pp. 118–121). School support teams are a vehicle for assisting schools as they plan and implement schoolwide programs. As you read and discuss the article, your study group might consider (a) aspects of school support teams that can strengthen the school reform process, (b) whether or not your school might benefit from a school support team, and (c) how your school might access or design a system of support for schoolwide planning and implementation.

PROMISING PRACTICES THAT FOSTER INCLUSIVE EDUCATION
Alice Udvari-Solner and Jacqueline S. Thousand

The inclusive education movement has often been viewed as a separate initiative running parallel or even counter to other curricular and instructional reform efforts (Block and Haring 1992). We take a holistic rather than separatist viewpoint and propose that the innovative changes occurring in general education are the same kinds of changes required for effective inclusion.

A number of established and emerging general education practices emulate the principles of inclusive education. When these practices are used, educators may be better equipped to facilitate meaningful and effective inclusive education for students perceived as disabled, at risk, or gifted, as well as those considered "average." Among the initiatives that have great promise for building inclusive schools are outcome-based education, multicultural education, multiple intelligence theory, constructivist learning, interdisciplinary curriculum, community-referenced instruction, authentic assessment of student performance, multi-age grouping, use of technology in the classroom, peer-mediated instruction, teaching responsibility and peacemaking, and collaborative teaming among adults and students. The remainder of this chapter examines each practice in the light of inclusive education.

Outcome-Based Education

Outcome-based education (OBE) is not a new concept to educators; it has evolved over the past 40 years to its current conceptualization with three central premises (Spady and Marshall 1991):

• All children can learn and succeed, although not in the same way or on the same day.

• Success breeds success.

• Schools determine the conditions of success.

In addition, OBE is guided by four principles (Brandt 1992/1993). The first, *clarity of focus,* implies that all aspects of education (curriculum, instruction, assessment) are centered on what we want children to demonstrate by the end of their schooling career (for example, the Circle of Courage outcomes of belonging, mastery, independence, and generosity discussed in Chapter 3). Everyone is clear at all times about the goals of education.

The second principle, *expanding opportunity,* recognizes that students learn in different ways and at different rates, and that various methods and contexts (perhaps out of the school building) are needed to optimize learning. Outcome demonstration is not tied to the calendar.

The third principle, *high expectations,* is rooted in the assumption that every student is "able to do significant things well" (Bill Spady, quoted by Brandt 1992/1993, p. 66). All students are expected to demonstrate success in their own way.

Finally, the fourth principle, *designing down,* turns the traditional method of designing curriculum upside down. Long-range outcomes are established first, and then curriculum is designed, always with an eye on where students ultimately are expected to end up.

Why institute OBE for students with disabilities? Clearly, OBE is consistent with and supportive of an inclusive education philosophy. OBE professes to encompass all students and focus on success for all. Additionally, many community members and education leaders are attracted to the autonomy schools are given to establish the means—the curriculum—for achieving significant outcomes. Teachers are encouraged to be flexible and to provide educational experiences in a variety of ways for a diverse student body. Students are not required to do the same things in the same ways in the same amount of time as same-aged peers.

Some question how students with severe disabilities can be included in OBE. McLaughlin and

Source: Reprinted from *Creating an Inclusive School,* edited by R. A. Villa and J. S. Thousand.
Copyright © 1995 by ASCD.

Warren (1992) argue that students with intensive challenges can be a part of the OBE model if the curriculum is defined in broad and balanced areas of knowledge and skill rather than narrow subject areas. To illustrate, 4,000 adults and students provided input into the development of Vermont's Common Core of Learning (Vermont State Department of Education 1993). The Common Core identified these skills as vital results: communication, reasoning and problem solving, personal development, social responsibility, and fields of knowledge including technology and new disciplines that "may be only just coming into existence" (p. 12).

Clearly, students with severe disabilities can achieve in many of these vital domains, although the performance criteria and method of assessing success may be quite different from that of their classmates. Central to this question is the notion of "personal best" (Shriner, Ysseldyke, Thurlow, and Honetschlager 1994, p. 41). For example, literacy may be an expectation for all graduates. One student demonstrates his personal best by writing a persuasive speech, whereas another demonstrates her personal best by effectively using her assistive communication device to express her wants and interests.

Multicultural Education

The term *multicultural education* has been used to describe various policies related to educational equity and practices that foster understanding of human differences and similarities (Banks and McGee Banks 1989, Sleeter and Grant 1994). The principles of multiculturalism were formulated in the 1960s and '70s as issues of culture and diversity rose to the forefront of political and educational arenas. Initially, these principles were most prominently associated with gender, ethnicity, and class distinctions. Only recently have the issues of disability and sexual orientation made their way into the multicultural literature (Tiedt and Tiedt 1990). As a result, multicultural education has rarely been linked effectively with inclusive education.

When the underlying goals of a multicultural approach are examined, they fit well with the ideological framework of inclusive education. The goals and outcomes of multicultural education are to:
- foster human rights and respect for difference,
- acknowledge the value of cultural diversity,
- promote an understanding of alternative life choices,
- establish social justice and equal opportunity, and
- facilitate equitable power distribution among individuals and groups (Gollnick 1980).

When school communities employ a multicultural approach, they make a commitment to empower students and to attempt to increase academic achievement by redesigning the entire educational agenda to make learning environments responsive to students' cultures, behavior, and learning styles (Banks and McGee Banks 1989).

Grant and Sleeter (1989) have extended the concept of multicultural education using a *reconstructionist* viewpoint. Simply stated, reconstructionism requires a critique of contemporary culture and a reconceptualization of what it can and should be to realize a more humane society (Brameld 1956). Students are encouraged to critically evaluate inequities and instances of discrimination or bias and to identify strategies for change. By engaging in a meta-analysis of existing conditions and establishing visions that reflect a value system, even the youngest members of school communities are encouraged to make a personal commitment to change. A reconstructionist orientation holds promise for accelerating educational reform by embedding reformation in teachers' and students' day-to-day discourse.

Although multicultural education and inclusion are not synonymous, administrators, educators, and community members need to recognize the commonalities between them so they may coordinate reform activities within schools to maximize the use of resources and optimize the number of children who will benefit.

Multiple Intelligences Theory

The theory of multiple intelligences (MI-theory) proposed by Howard Gardner (1983) questions the adequacy and efficacy of the traditional conceptualization of knowledge, aptitude, and intellect. As defined in the western world, intelligence has long been equated with logical and linguistic abilities. The underlying assumptions of this view are that the processes of the mind are quantifiable and can be translated into a singular construct. Furthermore, all children can be compared and rank ordered by intellectual prowess (Goldman and Gardner 1989), hence our reliance on I.Q. scores as essential descriptors of students' abilities and predictors of academic success.

MI-theory is based on the supposition that several distinct forms or families of intelligence exist—or, more accurately, co-exist—to create a constellation of ability for any one individual. Gardner (1983) has recommended consideration of at least seven types of intelligence: linguistic, logical-mathematical, musical, spatial, bodily-kinesthetic, interpersonal, and intrapersonal.

These categories are constructed to promote the valuing of skills beyond the conventional representations of verbal ability, written expression, and mathematical reasoning. Gardner's valued capacities include: the ability to depict and manipulate spatial representations; to think in and produce musical forms; to use kinesthetic action to perform, produce, and problem solve; and to use effective communication and interaction skills to understand others or reflect on one's own behavior.

The notion of multiple intelligences has important implications for inclusive education. Gardner based his theory in part on observations and studies of the capacities of children with disabilities and on the meaning of intelligence in varied cultures (Gardner 1983), thus validating a broader perspective. Teachers equipped with this perspective are in the position to appreciate students' "unconventional" behavior and seek productive applications of these skills within a learning context. They will arrange learning activities to allow expression of knowledge through multiple modes and the use of different intelligences. Teachers may use the student's strongest modalities or intelligences as vehicles to promote skill acquisition in weaker areas of performance.

MI-theory does not allow the student to be viewed only through the constricted lens of logic or language. Instead, learning and memory are seen as multifaceted and not completely understood. Consequently, our mechanisms for assessing intelligence are at the very least far too narrow and perhaps misguided. This calls into question the current systems used to identify and label any child as disabled. Embracing the tenets of MI-theory could interrupt the vicious cycle of labeling and the social construction of disability based on one or two aspects of ability. The use of a multiple-intelligence orientation liberates educators to see the idiosyncrasies in learning styles and differentiate curriculum for all students, thus making "difference" usual in the classroom.

Constructivist Learning

From a constructivist perspective, learning is the creation of meaning when an individual makes linkages between new knowledge and the context of existing knowledge (Poplin and Stone 1992). A key characteristic of this view, then, is that learners "construct" their own knowledge (Peterson, Fennema, and Carpenter 1988/1989). Generally speaking, the ideas of Brownwell, Vygotsky, Dewey, and Piaget are constructivist (Resnick and Klopfer 1989); underpinning their theories is the idea that knowledge is not quantitative but interpretive and must develop in social contexts of communities and communicative interchanges (Peterson and Knapp 1993).

Constructivism challenges the assumptions and practices of reductionism that have pervaded our educational practices for generations. In a deficit-driven reductionist framework, effective learning takes place in a rigid, hierarchical progression. Each concept or skill is broken into small segments or steps, and students learn each one in sequence (Poplin and Stone 1992). A supposition exists that children are unable to learn higher-order skills before mastering those of lower order (Peterson et al. 1988/1989). Learning, then, is an accumulation of isolated facts. It is presumed that through this accumulation process, learners will build skills and generate new knowledge.

Conceptualizing curriculum and instruction from a constructivist vantage point intersects productively with the practices of inclusive education. Constructivism fosters the idea that all people are always learning, and the process cannot be stopped (Poplin and Stone 1992). "No human being understands everything; every human being understands some thing. Education should strive to improve understanding as much as possible, whatever the student's proclivities might be" (Siegel and Shaughnessy 1994, p. 564). Both of these statements imply that there are few, if any, prerequisites for learning and that children must be met at their current level of performance without undue focus on remediation. It is acknowledged that all students enter school with different knowledge that is influenced by background, experiences, and cultural practice. Consequently, teachers must take into account these factors and ensure that new information is related in meaningful ways to each learner's existing knowledge.

Interdisciplinary Curriculum

An interdisciplinary approach is a curricular orientation that expressly employs methodology and language from more than one discipline to examine a central theme, issue, problem, topic, or experience (Jacobs 1989). Teachers and students are encouraged in a learning partnership to examine one area in depth from complex and multiple perspectives. Interdisciplinary curriculum may be implemented in several ways. At the elementary level, a single teacher can interface the content of assorted disciplines throughout one unit of study. Instructors of art, music, and physical education can further infuse the theme across the instructional day. Most true to the interdisciplinary philosophy is the practice at middle and high school levels of uniting teachers of separate disciplines to team teach around a selected set of issues.

Interdisciplinary/thematic approaches have grown out of dissatisfaction with discipline-based or subject-driven methods of curriculum organization. Discipline-based models are premised on the teaching of content knowledge. However, knowledge in all areas of study is growing exponentially each day. Essentially, there are not enough hours in the day to teach all that is new. Jacobs (1989) believes this indicates a need to rethink the way we select areas of study, deciding not only what should be taught, but what should be eliminated. Fragmentation of schedules and subject matter into allotted time periods is common practice in discipline-based approaches. With thematic methods, students are not forced to create bridges among seemingly unrelated splinters of information but instead can view issues in a holistic manner.

If discipline-based approaches pose drawbacks for the typical population, the impact on students with disabilities is likely to be more significant. One reason students with disabilities failed in the past in general education classes was that the subject matter presented was unrelated, out of context, and practiced only a few minutes per day without consideration for generalization and transfer. A thematic orientation offers a way to show how different subject areas relate and influence students' lives, thereby affirming the relevance of the curriculum (Ackerman and Perkins 1989, Bean 1990).

Community-Referenced Instruction

Community-referenced or community-based instruction is characterized by students applying skills in nonschool settings that have some relationship, relevance, and purpose to their lives now or in the future (Falvey 1989). Instruction takes place regularly in community environments where age-appropriate vocational, domestic, community, or recreational skills can be acquired (Brown, Branston, Baumgart, Vincent, Falvey, and Schroeder 1979). The premise behind community-referenced instruction is that all students need an education that prepares them with the skills to live and work as part of the adult community—in other words, to achieve functional outcomes (Clark 1994).

A community-based approach to instruction evolved as a best practice for students with moderate and severe disabilities (Brown et al. 1979). However, it is now recognized as a valuable tool in the education of all students (Peterson, LeRoy, Field, and Wood 1992). Given the complexities of adult life in the 21st century, educators are realizing that all the skills that are relevant, critical, and enriching cannot be taught effectively within the confines of the classroom. For students with significant disabilities who may experience problems generalizing skills acquired in one setting to another, the need for systematic instruction in the actual environment of concern is evident. For students without disabilities, there is a need to connect with the larger community, work in concert with community members to engage in problem-solving skills, and integrate themselves as participants in businesses and organizations long before graduation occurs.

Accessing the community for instruction can provide a student with disabilities the context to learn or maintain a new skill. The same environment can be used as a "fidelity check" for the application of math, science, or language skills for typical students. For example, each week a group of three students from a 7th grade home economics class goes to the local grocery store. For the member of the group who has disabilities, the weekly trip serves as an opportunity to learn to travel by city bus, cross streets, and select and pay for groceries. The other students in the group must use mathematics and nutrition skills by comparative shopping to select items that are most economical and contain the least grams of fat, thus employing skills emphasized within the classroom.

Authentic Assessment of Student Performance

The need for better alignment between assessment and instruction is even more evident (Chittenden 1991) as schools have begun to shift their curriculum to include multicultural, constructivist, interdisciplinary, and community-referenced approaches, and as teachers have placed more emphasis on the meaning of learning with attention to children's interests and proclivities. Traditional measures of performance that do not provide information about students' understanding and quality of thinking are out of step with dynamic, student-centered instructional practices.

Perrone (1994) noted that typical assessment techniques relying primarily on the recall of knowledge provide an artificial, decontextualized view of the learner. Assessment has been equated with the possession of information rather than the acquisition of global constructs (e.g., learning the process of writing) (Zessoules and Gardner 1991). In most cases, data acquired from these assessments are unrelated to the ways students naturally learn or will need to use the knowledge. This problem is amplified for students with disabilities. When traditional measures such as standardized, norm-referenced tests are used for evaluation, their performances predictably fall below those of their nondisabled peers. Thus, a unidimensional and deficit-oriented profile of the learner is maintained.

Based on the need for more realistic and responsive outcome measures, a number of alternative evaluation techniques—authentic assessments—have evolved. Authentic assessment occurs when students are expected to perform, produce, or otherwise demonstrate skills that represent realistic learning demands (Choate and Evans 1992, Diez and Moon 1992). According to Meyer (1992), the contexts of the assessments are real-life settings in and out of the classroom without contrived and standardized conditions. Authentic assessments can be considered exhibitions of learning that are gathered over time to show evidence of progress, acquisition, and application. For example, written expression may be assessed through the use of a portfolio that includes several samples of writing representing conceptual ideas, rough drafts, self-edited papers, and final versions. Included in this assessment may be products such as poems, letters, or research papers that illustrate ability to use other forms of written expression. The student also is encouraged to include self-evaluations and personal goals for progress.

Common features of authentic assessments are:

• Students must integrate and apply skills to accomplish a larger task (Choate and Evans 1992).

• The processes of learning, higher-level thinking, or problem-solving are emphasized, as well as the product of these actions (Diez and Moon 1992).

• Assessment tasks must help students make judgments about their own performance. Through self-appraisal, children set goals for progress and provoke further learning (Perrone 1994, Zessoules and Gardner 1991).

• The criteria for performance are negotiated and made explicit to students in advance (Wiggins 1989).

The use of authentic assessments is an important component in creating inclusive classrooms. This form of evaluation is closely linked to the individualized, performance-based assessment that has been the preferred mode of assessment in special education. These techniques are less likely to be culturally biased for students who are limited in English proficiency or in any other intellectual, physical, or emotional capacity.

Students with unique learning characteristics and their peers are allowed to express knowledge through multiple modes and in nontraditional ways (Perrone 1991). Instruction and assessments are provided with relevant tasks so students who have difficulty generalizing skills or using them out of context are not required to transfer learnings to demonstrate understanding (Choate and Evans 1992). Functional expressions of competence more

readily enable teachers to identify skills that are discrepant or mastered, thus giving direction to instruction of highest priority.

Multi-Age Grouping

Kasten and Clarke (1993) define multi-age grouping as "any deliberate grouping of children that includes more than one traditional grade level in a single classroom community" (p. 3). Also referred to as nongraded, family, or vertical grouping, multi-age classrooms are considered single learning communities made up of a balanced collection of students from the school population with consideration for heterogeneity in gender, ability, ethnicity, interests, and age levels. It is not unlikely to have siblings and members of the extended family within one vertical grouping.

The multi-age classroom, a well-established practice in countries such as Canada, New Zealand, Britain, and some parts of the United States (Elkind 1987), is based on several underlying assumptions that directly oppose the traditional practice of grade-level grouping. Grade-level grouping presumes that students who are the same age have like learning needs and abilities, thus benefiting from similar instruction. Placement of the child is based solely on age or physical time (Elkind 1987). Learning by grade level is viewed as a predictable, sequential, and orderly procedure; and one year of schooling is a product that can be judged and rated by a standard of performance (Kasten and Clark 1993).

In contrast, a multi-age approach is based on the assumption that learning is a continuous and dynamic process. Student diversity is essential. Children are expected and, in fact, encouraged to learn at different rates and levels. The growth of the child is viewed in both biological and psychological time, rather than merely physical time, so that learning experiences are designed as developmentally appropriate.

Many elements of multi-age grouping that work for students without disabilities are also advantageous for students with disabilities. The emphasis on *heterogeneity* requires a classroom organization flexible enough to accommodate children at different levels of maturity and with different levels of intellectual ability. In fact, diversity impedes the use of lock-step instructional methods aimed at the whole class or a specific grade level.

The sense of *community* created over time among teachers and students is advantageous to promote long-term networks of support for students with disabilities. Transitions from setting to setting and teacher to teacher are associated with recoupment, generalization, and social adjustment difficulties for some students with disabilities. These "passages" are reduced in nongraded groupings, and teachers have time to get to know a particular student. Teachers can use information gained about the child in one year to plan learning experiences for the next year without the risk of losing that knowledge in a transition to new staff.

Use of Technology in the Classroom

Technology is proving to be a catalyst for transforming schooling by fostering excitement in learning for all children. As Peck and Dorricott of the Institute for the Reinvention of Education (1994) observed:

To see students so engaged in learning that they lose track of time, to see a level of excitement that causes students to come to school early and stay late, and to have time to develop strong relationships with students and to meet their individual needs allows educators to fulfill age-old dreams (p. 14).

What is technology? It is more than computers and software packages, and it reinvents itself almost daily. Technology in education includes calculators, video cameras, VCRs, portable personal computers, printers, general-purpose software such as word processing programs and *HyperCard*, computer-assisted instruction for drill and practice, laser videodisks, telecommunication networks such as electronic mail, distance education, interactive multimedia, scanners, text-to-speech and speech-to-text software, pen-based notepads such as the Apple *Newton*, and more. Given the current and expanding access to technology inside and outside of the classroom, the climate is conducive to including students with disabilities who need technology to access the curriculum, express their knowledge, communicate, or control their environment.

In the past, technology was only in the possession of a few experts such as the computer lab teacher or those who designed or programmed augmentative communication systems for students with communication limitations. Today, technology has become "user friendly." Educators are joining the ranks of adults and children who rarely go a day without interacting with their laptop computer for desktop publishing, data management, game playing, or instantly communicating and socializing via the Internet.

Technological tools of a student with disabilities that once seemed too complex, cumbersome, or expensive (for example, massive computers bolted to a table or voice synthesizers) have become very portable, affordable, and standard hardware and software features of schools. Technology that used to be unusual for a single student now is usual within the classroom. Never before have educators been in such an ideal position to capitalize on technological advances in order to readily educate students who have different learning styles and rates or who rely on technological support to learn, communicate, and control their world.

In an interview with Frank Betts (1994), David Thornburg laid out a scenario that would equip every 2nd or 3rd grade child with a "loaded" computer for $100 per child. For $200, the system could be upgraded in 8th grade. But he cautions that even with the feasibility for advanced technology at every child's fingertips at home and school, equipment and software do not guarantee an excellent educational program (Thornburg 1992). Teachers still need to get to know each child and base decisions on how each child learns. Commenting on the use of technology to support the inclusion and learning of students with disabilities in school, Dutton and Dutton (1990) state it this way:

Remember that technology is not a "cure" for a disability; rather, it is a tool for everyone in society. Focus should not be placed on how the equipment itself will work, but efforts should be placed toward developing strategies, utilizing effective teaching practices, and working with the strengths of all students in the class. Technology can help remove barriers, but it is people, working together, who learn and succeed (p. 182).

Chapter 6 offers a process for interprofessional collaboration to adapt curriculum and instruction that may include the use of technology to meet individual student needs.

Peer-Mediated Instruction

"Peer-mediated instruction" (Harper, Maheady, and Mallette 1994, p. 229) refers to any teaching arrangement in which students serve as instructional agents for other students. Cooperative group-learning models and peer tutoring or partner learning strategies are two forms of peer-mediated instruction that support inclusive education.

As Johnson and Johnson (1994) point out, students may interact in three ways during learning. They may compete to see who is the best, they may work alone and individually toward their goals without attending to other students, or they may have a stake in one another's success by working cooperatively. Competitive learning interferes with community building, which is one objective of inclusive education. Yet, "research indicates that a vast majority of students in the United States view school as a competitive enterprise where one tries to do better than other students" (Johnson and Johnson 1994, pp. 32–33).

It is critical to note the dramatic difference between simply asking students to sit together and work in a group, and careful structuring so students work in cooperative learning groups. A group of children chatting together at a table as they do their own work is not a cooperative group, because no sense of positive interdependence exists, and no need for mutual support is arranged for them. It is only under particular conditions that groups will have healthy and productive relationships and may be expected to be more productive than in individualistic or competitive learning arrangements. Common to the diverse approaches of cooperative learning are five conditions or attributes:

• a joint task or learning activity suitable for group work,

• small-group learning in teams of five or fewer members,

• a focus on cooperative interpersonal behaviors,

• positive interdependence through team members' encouragement of one another's learning, and

• individual responsibility and accountability for the participation and learning of each team member (Davidson 1994).

A rich research base supports the use of cooperative learning to facilitate successful learning in heterogeneous groupings of students with varying abilities, interests, and backgrounds. Within the context of inclusive education, cooperative learning makes great sense as an instructional strategy as it enables students "to learn and work in environments where their individual strengths are recognized and individual needs are addressed" (Sapon-Shevin, Ayres, and Duncan 1994, p. 46). In other words, cooperative learning allows the classroom to be transformed into a microcosm of the diverse society and work world into which students will enter and a place for acquiring the skills to appreciate and cope with people who initially might be perceived as different or even difficult. Within this context, students learn what a society in which each person is valued would be like.

Partner learning or peer tutoring systems are not new; teachers of one-room school houses relied heavily on students as instructors. Children are continually teaching one another informally when they play games and engage in sports. Partner learning systems build relationships among students and offer a cost-effective way of enhancing engaged learning time on the part of children. Peer tutor systems can be same-age or cross-age and can be established within a single classroom, across classes, or across an entire school. Evidence of the social, instructional, and cost effectiveness of tutoring continues to mount (e.g., Fuchs, Fuchs, Hamlett, Phillips, and Bentz 1994; Thousand, Villa, and Nevin 1994). Benefits to students receiving this type of instruction include learning gains, interpersonal skill development, and heightened self-esteem. Good and Brophy (1987) suggest the quality of instruction provided by trained tutors may be superior to that of adults for at least three reasons:

• Children use more age-appropriate and meaningful language and examples.

• Having recently learned what they are to teach, they are familiar with their partner's potential frustrations.

• They tend to be more direct than adults.

Tutors also experience benefits similar to those of their partners. Namely, they develop interpersonal skills and may enhance self-esteem. Further, tutors report that they understand the concepts, procedures, and operations they teach at a much deeper level than they did before instructing. This likely is due to their meta-cognitive activity when preparing to teach.

Teaching Responsibility and Peacemaking

Among the children who are perceived as the most challenging to educate within current school organizational structures are those who demonstrate high rates of rule-violating behavior, children who have acquired maladaptive ways of relating, and children who are perceived as troubled or troubling. Adversity at home and in the community negatively affects an increasing number of children's ability and motivation to learn. The educator's job has broadened from providing effective and personalized

learning opportunities to addressing the stressors in children's lives by offering a variety of school-based social supports (for example, breakfast program, free lunch, mental health, and other human services on campus). Personal responsibility and peacemaking have risen to the top as curriculum priorities (Villa, Udis, and Thousand 1994).

Educators long have recognized that for students to master a content area such as mathematics or science, they need continuous and complex instruction throughout their elementary, middle, and high school years. When a child does not grasp concept or skill, we react with a "teaching response" and attempt to reteach the material with additional or different supports and accommodations. The content area of responsibility, however, has not received the same immediate treatment. The explicit teaching of patterns of behavior and habits representative of responsible behavior often never occurs. Instead, instruction is relegated to reactive, add on, quick-fix methods such as seeing a guidance counselor, going to a six-week social skills group, or instituting a written behavior change plan. To teach responsibility is as demanding as teaching any other content; it requires careful thought and complex, ongoing instruction from the day a child enters school.

Requisite to students learning responsible values, attitudes, and behaviors is the perception that somebody in the school community genuinely cares about them. Thus, teachers, above all, must demonstrate caring and concern by validating students' efforts and achievements. They must also directly teach responsibility by setting limits to ensure safety; establishing a schoolwide discipline system that promotes the learning of responsibility; and directly instructing students in pro-social communication skills, anger management, and impulse control techniques (Villa et al. 1994).

Models of discipline that are responsibility based (Curwin and Mendler 1988, Glasser 1986) acknowledge conflict as a natural part of life. They consider behavior to be contextual and transform the educator's role from cop to facilitator. There are no "if-then" consequences (e.g., three tardies equals a detention; 10 absences results in a grade of "F" in the missed class). Instead, responses to rule-violating behavior depend on all kinds of factors such as the time of day, the frequency and intensity of the behavior, and the number of other people exhibiting the behavior. These responses range from reminders, warnings, re-directions, cues, and self-monitoring techniques to behavioral contracts and direct teaching of alternative responses. Most important is to recognize that the development of student responsibility should be part of the curriculum and considered as important as any other curriculum domain. It should be concerned with teaching young people how to get their needs met in socially acceptable ways and should include modeling, coaching, and ongoing thought and reflection on the part of school personnel.

One way to incorporate the development of student responsibility into the curriculum and culture of a school is to turn conflict management back to the students by using them as peer mediators. In an increasing number of North American schools, students are trained to mediate conflicts and are available during school hours to conduct mediations at student, teacher, or administrator request. A small number of students may be selected and trained in mediation processes or all students may receive training in conflict resolutions skills. Students who serve as mediators sometimes are called peacemakers or conflict managers.

Schrumpf (1994) outlined a structured process for establishing a peer mediation program within a school. He emphasizes that peer mediation must be made highly visible so students and teachers actually use the program as an alternative to adult intervention. Mediators need ongoing adult support through regular meetings in which they discuss issues and receive advanced training. Data collection in the form of Peer Mediation Requests and Peer Mediation Agreements are analyzed to determine the nature, frequency, and outcomes of mediation requests.

Emerging data suggest that peer mediation programs correlate with improved school attendance and decreases in fights, student suspensions, and vandalism. For example, of the 130 teachers in a New York City school in which students practiced peer mediation, 71 percent reported reductions in physical violence, 66 percent heard less verbal harassment, and 69 percent observed increased student willingness to cooperate with one another (Meek 1992). Learning to resolve conflicts with peers is an empowering action consistent with the principles of inclusive education, with the potential of generalizing from peace between two people to peacemaking in community and global contexts.

Collaborative Teaming Among Adults and Students

As emphasized in the preceding chapter, schools showing great success in responding to student diversity have redefined the role of general and special educators and other support personnel to that of collaborative team members who assemble to jointly problem solve the daily challenges of heterogeneous schooling. Among the benefits of collaborative planning and teaching team arrangements is the increased instructor/learner ratio and the resulting immediacy in diagnosing and responding to individual student's needs. Teaming arrangements capitalize on the diverse knowledge and instructional strengths of each team member and, when special educators are included on the team, eliminate the need to refer students to special education in order to access special educators' support. Although "collaborative teaming" is not yet the norm in North American schools, when the term is discussed, it generally conjures up images of adults (usually professional educators, sometimes community members) sharing planning, teaching, and evaluation responsibilities. Until recently, the students themselves were missing from the teaming concept.

Villa and Thousand (1992) have identified multiple rationales for including students in collaborative educational roles with adults. First, students represent a wealthy pool of expertise, refreshing creativity, and enthusiasm at no cost to schools. Second, educational reform recommendations call for students to exercise higher-level thinking skills to determine what, where, when, and how they will learn. Third, collaborating with adults in advocacy efforts for other learners helps students develop the ethic and practice of contributing to and caring for a greater community and society. Fourth, given the information explosion and the complexity of our networked global community, collaborative teaming skills are necessary for survival in the workplace. Educators, then, have a responsibility to model collaboration by sharing their decision-making and instructional power with students and arranging for and inviting students to join in at least the following collaborative endeavors (Villa and Thousand 1992):

- Students as members of teaching teams and as instructors in cooperative learning and partner learning arrangements.

- Students as members of planning teams, determining accommodations for themselves or classmates with and without disabilities.

- Students functioning as advocates for themselves and for classmates during meetings (e.g., individual educational plan meeting for a student with a disability) and other major events that determine a student's future educational and post-school choices.

- Students as mediators of conflict.

- Students providing social and logistical support to a classmate as a peer partner or a member of a Circle of Friends (Falvey, Forest, Pearpoint, and Rosenberg 1994).

- Students as coaches of their teachers, offering feedback regarding the effectiveness of their instructional and discipline procedures and decisions.

- Students as members of inservice, curriculum, discipline, and other school governance committees such as the school board.

All of these options for collaboration facilitate meaningful inclusion and participation of students with disabilities in school. Asking students to join with adults in collaborative action is a critical strategy for fostering the spirit of community and equity that is foundational to quality heterogeneous schooling experiences and the desired educational outcomes of active student participation and critical thinking.

The exemplary and promising practices identified in this chapter establish the infrastructure within which the principles of inclusive education can be realized. Collectively, the initiatives have the potential to a create a unified philosophy and revolutionary standards of educational practice. The success of any change, however, always relies on the courage and determination of practicing educators to translate and put in place principles of these contemporary reform initiatives. "You can't mandate what matters," Fullan writes (1993, p. 125); instead, the complex goals of change require knowledge, skills, collaboration, creative thinking, and committed and passionate action. If widespread progress is ever to occur in education, inclusive education must not be treated as an "add on" to other pressing initiatives; it must be the central discussion, and teachers must be the central participants in a scholarly discourse on education's future. The interface between inclusive education and other exemplary practices must become clearly and publicly self-evident (Peterson and Knapp 1993).

References

Ackerman, D., and D.N. Perkins. (1989). "Integrating Thinking and Learning Skills Across the Curriculum." In *Interdisciplinary Curriculum: Design and Implementation,* edited by H.H. Jacobs. Alexandria Va: Association for Supervision and Curriculum Development.

Banks, J., and C. McGee Banks. (1989). *Multicultural Education: Issues and Perspectives.* Boston: Allyn and Bacon.

Bean, J. (May 1990). "Rethinking the Middle School Curriculum." *Middle School Journal* 21, 5: 1–5.

Betts, F. (1994). "On the Birth of the Communication Age: A Conversation with David Thornburg." *Educational Leadership* 51, 7: 20–23.

Block, J.H., and T.G. Haring. (1992). "On Swamps, Bogs, Alligators and Special Education Reform." In *Restructuring for a Caring and Effective Education: An Adminis-*

trative Guide to Creating Heterogeneous Education, edited by R. Villa, J. Thousand, W. Stainback, and S. Stainback. Baltimore: Paul H. Brookes.

Brameld, T. (1956). *Toward a Reconstructed Philosophy of Education.* New York: Holt, Rinehart, and Winston.

Brandt, R. (1992/1993). "A Conversation with Bill Spady." *Educational Leadership* 50, 4: 66–70.

Brown, L., M. Branston, D. Baumgart, L. Vincent, M. Falvey, and J. Schroeder. (1979). "Utilizing the Characteristics of Current and Subsequent Environments as Factors in the Development of Curricular Content for Severely Handicapped Students." *AAESPH Review* 4, 4: 407–424.

Chittenden, E. (1991). "Authentic Assessment, Evaluation, and Documentation." In *Expanding Student Assessment,* edited by V. Perrone. Alexandria, Va.: Association for Supervision and Curriculum Development.

Choate, J.S., and S. Evans. (1992). "Authentic Assessment of Special Learners: Problem or Promise?" *Preventing School Failure* 37, 1: 6–9.

Clark, G. (1994). "Is Functional Curriculum Approach Compatible with an Inclusive Education Model?" *Teaching Exceptional Children* 26, 2: 36–37.

Curwin, R., and A. Mendler. (1988). *Discipline with Dignity.* Alexandria, Va.: Association for Supervision and Curriculum Development.

Davidson, N. (1994). "Cooperative and Collaborative Learning: An Integrated Perspective." In *Creativity and Collaborative Learning: A Practical Guide to Empowering Students and Teachers,* edited by J. Thousand, R. Villa, and A. Nevin. Baltimore: Paul H. Brookes.

Diez, M., and J. Moon. (1992). "What Do We Want Students to Know? . . . And Other Important Questions." *Educational Leadership* 49, 8: 38–41.

Dutton, D.H., and D.L. Dutton. (1990). "Technology to Support Diverse Needs in Regular Classes." In *Support Networks for Inclusive Schooling: Interdependent Integrated Education,* edited by W. Stainback and S. Stainback. Baltimore: Paul H. Brookes.

Elkind, D. (1987). "Multiage Grouping." *Young Children* 43, 11: 2.

Falvey, M.A. (1989). *Community Based Curriculum: Instructional Strategies for Students with Severe Handicaps.* Baltimore: Paul H. Brookes.

Falvey, M.A., M. Forest, J. Pearpoint, and R.L. Rosenberg. (1994). "Building Connections." In *Creativity and Collaborative Learning: A Practical Guide to Empowering Students and Teachers,* edited by J. Thousand, R. Villa, and A. Nevin. Baltimore: Paul H. Brookes.

Ford, A., R. Schnorr, L. Meyer, L. Davern, J. Black, and P. Dempsey. (1989). *The Syracuse Community-Referenced Curriculum Guide for Students with Moderate and Severe Disabilities.* Baltimore: Paul H. Brookes.

Fuchs, L.S., D. Fuchs, C.L. Hamlett, N.B. Phillips, and J. Bentz. (1994). "Classwide Curriculum-Based Measurement: Helping General Educators Meet the Challenge of Student Diversity." *Exceptional Children* 60: 518–537.

Fullan, M. (1993). "Innovative Reform and Restructuring Strategies." In *Challenges and Achievements of American Education,* edited by G. Cawelti. 1993 ASCD Yearbook. Alexandria, Va.: Association for Supervision and Curriculum Development.

Gardner, H. (1983). *Frames of Mind: The Theory of Multiple Intelligences.* New York: Harper Collins Publishers.

Glasser, W. (1986). *Control Theory in the Classroom.* New York: Harper and Row.

Goldman, J., and H. Gardner. (1989). "Multiple Paths to Educational Effectiveness." In *Beyond Separate Education: Quality Education for All,* edited by D.K. Lipskey and A. Gartner. Baltimore: Paul H. Brookes.

Gollnick, D.M. (1980). "Multicultural Education." *Viewpoints in Teaching and Learning* 56: 1–17.

Good, T.L., and J.G. Brophy. (1987). *Looking into Classrooms,* 4th ed. New York: Harper & Row.

Grant, C., and C. Sleeter. (1989). "Race, Class, Gender, Exceptionality, and Educational Reform." In *Multicultural Education: Issues and Perspectives,* edited by J. Banks and C. McGee Banks. Boston: Allyn and Bacon.

Harper, G.F., L. Maheady, and B. Mallette. (1994). "The Power of Peer-Mediated Instruction: How and Why It Promotes Academic Success for All Students." In *Creativity and Collaborative Learning: A Practical Guide to Empowering Students and Teachers,* edited by J. Thousand, R. Villa, and A. Nevin. Baltimore: Paul H. Brookes.

Jacobs, H.H. (1989). "The Growing Need for Interdisciplinary Curriculum Content." In *Interdisciplinary Curriculum: Design and Implementation,* edited by H.H. Jacobs. Alexandria Va.: Association for Supervision and Curriculum Development.

Johnson, R.T., and D.W. Johnson. (1994). "An Overview of Cooperative Learning." In *Creativity and Collaborative Learning: A Practical Guide to Empowering Students and Teachers,* edited by J. Thousand, R. Villa, and A. Nevin. Baltimore: Paul H. Brookes.

Kasten, W., and B. Clarke. (1993). *The Multi-age Classroom: A Family of Learners.* Katonah, N.Y.: Richard C. Owen Publishers.

McLaughlin, M., and S. Warren. (1992). *Issues and Options in Restructuring Schools and Special Education Programs.* College Park: University of Maryland, The Center for Policy Options in Special Education, and the Institute for the Study of Exceptional Children and Youth.

Meek, M. (Fall 1992). "The Peacekeepers." *Teaching Tolerance,* pp. 46–52.

Meyer, C. (1992). "What's the Difference Between Authentic and Performance Assessment?" *Educational Leadership* 49, 8: 39–40.

116

Peck, K., and D. Dorricott. (1994). "Why Use Technology?" *Educational Leadership* 15, 7: 11–14.

Perrone, V. (1991). *Expanding Student Assessment.* Alexandria, Va.: Association for Supervision and Curriculum Development.

Perrone, V. (1994). "How to Engage Students in Learning." *Educational Leadership* 51, 5: 11–13.

Peterson, M., B. LeRoy, S. Field, and P. Wood. (1992). "Community-Referenced Learning in Inclusive Schools: Effective Curriculum for All Students." In *Curriculum Considerations in Inclusive Classrooms: Facilitating Learning for All* (pp. 207–227), edited by S. Stainback and W. Stainback. Baltimore: Paul H. Brookes.

Peterson, P., E. Fennema, and T. Carpenter. (1988/1989). "Using Knowledge of How Students Think About Math." *Educational Leadership* 46, 4: 42–46.

Peterson, P., and N. Knapp. (1993). "Inventing and Reinventing Ideas: Constructivist Teaching and Learning in Mathematics." In *Challenges and Achievements of American Education,* edited by G. Cawelti. 1993 ASCD Yearbook. Alexandria, Va.: Association for Supervision and Curriculum Development.

Poplin, M.S., and S. Stone. (1992). "Paradigm Shifts in Instructional Strategies: From Reductionism to Holistic/Constructivism." In *Controversial Issues Confronting Special Education: Divergent Perspectives,* edited by W. Stainback and S. Stainback. Boston: Allyn and Bacon.

Resnick, L.B., and L.E. Klopfer. (1989). *Toward the Thinking Curriculum: Current Cognitive Research.* Alexandria, Va.: Association for Supervision and Curriculum Development.

Sapon-Shevin, M., B.J. Ayres, and J. Duncan. (1994). "Cooperative Learning and Inclusion." In *Creativity and Collaborative Learning: A Practical Guide to Empowering Students and Teachers,* edited by J. Thousand, R. Villa, and A. Nevin. Baltimore: Paul H. Brookes.

Schrumpf, F. (1994). "The Role of Students in Resolving Conflicts in Schools." In *Creativity and Collaborative Learning: A Practical Guide to Empowering Students and Teachers,* edited by J. Thousand, R. Villa, and A. Nevin. Baltimore: Paul H. Brookes.

Shriner, J.G., J.E. Ysseldyke, M.L. Thurlow, and D. Honetschlager. (1994). " 'All' Means 'All': Including Students with Disabilities." *Educational Leadership* 51, 6: 38–42.

Siegel, J., and M. Shaughnessy. (March 1994). "An Interview with Howard Gardner: Educating for Understanding." *Phi Delta Kappan* 75, 7: 563–566.

Sleeter, C., and C. Grant. (1994). 2nd ed. "Education That Is Multicultural and Social Reconstructionist." In *Making Choices for Multicultural Education: Five Approaches to Race, Class, and Gender,* edited by C. Sleeter and C. Grant. New York: Merrill.

Spady, W., and K. Marshall. (1991). "Beyond Traditional Outcome-Based Education." *Educational Leadership* 49, 2: 67–72.

Thornburg, D. (1992). *Edutrends 2010.* San Carlos, Calif.: Starsong Publications.

Thousand, J., R. Villa, and A. Nevin. (1994). *Creativity and Collaborative Learning: A Practical Guide to Empowering Students and Teachers.* Baltimore: Paul H. Brookes.

Tiedt, P., and I. Tiedt. (1990). 3rd ed. "Education for Multicultural Understanding." In *Multicultural Teaching: A Handbook of Activities, Information, and Resources,* edited by P. Tiedt and I. Tiedt. Boston: Allyn and Bacon.

Vermont State Department of Education. (1993). *Vermont's Common Core of Learning: The Results We Need from Education.* Montpelier, Vt.: Vermont State Department of Education.

Villa, R., and J. Thousand. (1992). "Student Collaboration: An Essential for Curriculum Delivery in the 21st Century." In *Curriculum Considerations in Inclusive Classrooms: Facilitating Learning for All Students,* edited by S. Stainback and W. Stainback. Baltimore: Paul H. Brookes.

Villa, R., J. Udis, and J. Thousand. (1994). "Responses for Children Experiencing Behavioral and Emotional Challenges." In *Creativity and Collaborative Learning: A Practical Guide to Empowering Students and Teachers,* edited by J. Thousand, R. Villa, and A. Nevin. Baltimore: Paul H. Brookes.

Wiggins, G. (1989). "Teaching to the (Authentic) Test." *Educational Leadership* 46, 7: 41–47.

Zessoules, R., and H. Gardner. (1991). "Authentic Assessment: Beyond the Buzzword and Into the Classroom." In *Expanding Student Assessment,* edited by V. Perrone. Alexandria, Va.: Association for Supervision and Curriculum Development.

Alice Udvari-Solner is Assistant Professor, Department of Curriculum and Instruction and Department of Rehabilitation Psychology and Special Education, University of Wisconsin-Madison, 255 N. Mill St., Room 2448, Madison, WI 53706.
Jacqueline S. Thousand is Research Associate Professor at the College of Education and Social Services and University Affiliated Facility, 449C Waterman Building, University of Vermont, Burlington, VT 05405.

BUILDING CAPACITY THROUGH SCHOOL SUPPORT TEAMS
Joseph F. Johnson Jr. and Margery Ginsberg

School support teams in Texas are helping schools rewrite the way Title I programs serve students in high-poverty schools.

Too often federal legislation dictates what educators do, how they do it, and what happens if it is not done. Rarely does legislation provide structures that build our capacity to improve teaching and learning in schools.

Title I of the Improving America's Schools Act is an exception. In addition to giving schools greater flexibility in the use of federal resources, the law now requires states to establish systems of intensive and sustained support for schools that receive Title I funds. The primary component of these systems is *school support teams* (Public Law 103-382, Section 1117c 1994).

These teams—external groups of teachers, pupil services personnel, and other people with expertise in school reform—assist schools as they plan, implement, and improve their schoolwide programs (Moffett 1996). (Under federal education law, high-poverty schools may use Title I and other federal education resources to support comprehensive school reform through schoolwide programs— that is, programs that integrate school planning and improvement activities in ways that increase the capacity of the entire school to ensure the academic success of all students. This is a break with traditional Title I/Chapter 1 approaches, which usually targeted auxiliary services exclusively to students who met district-defined eligibility criteria.)

School support teams provide support and assistance to the staff of high-poverty schools as they plan and develop these schoolwide programs. Because Congress clearly wanted schools to be thoughtful about their many options for improving teaching and learning, the law requires schools to spend a year planning their approach and to get outside help during the process. School support teams are designed to increase the likelihood that this new flexibility will lead to substantial increases in student achievement.

For the past two years, we have been working with educators in Texas to incorporate the school support team structure into the state's Title I approach. In the course of our work, we've learned some lessons that may prove helpful to other states and districts developing their own approaches to Title I programming, as well as to external change agents who are assisting schools with systemic change.

The Texas Initiative

The Texas School Support Team Initiative began with a pilot program during the 1994–95 school year and recently completed its first year of statewide implementation.

In the pilot, 12 high-poverty schools were invited to receive assistance from school support teams. Volunteers from education service centers, colleges and universities, and educators from high-achieving Title I schools formed a large pool of support team members from which participating schools could choose. A facilitator from the Texas Education Agency (the state's education department) chaired each support team. Every facilitator received training on a variety of topics, including school change processes, group facilitation skills, and relevant changes to Title I; members of the support team pool received a condensed version of the training.

All facilitators made a preliminary visit to their assigned school, during which they explained the purposes of the visit to the principal and other staff, planned the initial team visit, and selected the support team members from the pool they felt could lend the most targeted assistance.

A full-team visit was next. During the two-day visit, the support team met the school staff; toured the campus; interviewed teachers, support personnel, parents, and administrators individually or in small groups; and held a planning meeting at the end of the visit. The purpose of and approach to the visits varied slightly depending on the needs of the school. Usually, however, the initial full-team visit was structured to assist the school in the initial phases of its planning and to strengthen the foundation for the decisions staff would be making. After the visit, team members provided support by phone and helped school staff find materials and resources to assist them. The team also made a follow-up visit to further assist the school in its planning process.

Last year, the first year of large-scale implementation, Texas used several different models, coordinated by its 20 regional education service centers. The models respected local needs while building on the lessons learned in the pilot initiative. Thus, school support teams were organized differently, based on the resources of each education service center, the number of schools needing assistance, and the preferences of local administrators. The length of visits ranged from a half day to two days. Teams were led by service center staff, district-level personnel, or school-based educators.

What We've Learned

At this point, we've collected considerable feedback on the pilot initiative and the first year of large-scale implementation, through surveys, focus groups, and teleconferences. Based on our work in Texas and the data accumulated so far, we believe that the following considerations are critical to a support team's success:

1. Building trust. Important, lasting changes are most likely to occur in an atmosphere of openness and trust. If school personnel perceive the support team to be a group of monitors or investigators, they will maintain defensive postures. But if an atmosphere of trust and mutual respect is established, schools receiving assistance are more likely to openly share their concerns, fears, and dreams for the future.

We found that trust develops when everyone involved in the process clearly understands the purpose of a school support team, how a visit might be conducted, who might be involved, and why. Early, frequent, and clear communication is essential. A preliminary visit from a support team coordinator provides not only the opportunity to meet with school staff and negotiate a mutually acceptable agenda for the full-team visit, but allays fears that the support team process is designed to monitor the school.

The attitude of support team members is perhaps the most important factor in building trust. Support team members must convey respect for the accomplishments, challenges, and autonomy of the schools they support. They must demonstrate a commitment to listening more than talking, to observing more than reporting.

2. Starting with strengths. In school improvement, educators frequently focus on identifying needs or weaknesses. Yet, some promising school improvement models emphasize the importance of building on strengths (Levin 1991; Saxl et. al. 1989).

In Texas, school support teams encouraged school staffs to look at themselves from different perspectives. Staff members constructed portfolios or profiles to communicate their accomplishments, and some developed case studies of themselves to look for strengths they had not previously recognized. The support teams also helped schools to look anew at student achievement data and to identify accomplishments, even in areas where accomplishments were not readily apparent.

Support teams then helped school personnel conceptualize how they might build on those strengths and transfer them to other classrooms, grade levels, student groups, and curriculum areas.

This positive approach provided often-needed recognition for dedicated efforts, while encouraging growth in areas of need.

One school-based team developed a unique approach to identifying strengths and growth areas. They created a colorful metaphorical illustration in which "blooms" showed programs that were in place but still needed tending, "seeds" represented ideas for substantive change, "nutrients" identified what would have to happen for teaching and learning to improve for all students, "clouds" signified challenges school staff would have to overcome as they tried to change, and the "sun" depicted how members of the school community might sustain their energy as they continued to ask difficult questions about the work ahead. The illustration provided a nice context for looking at the whole picture of what the school believed about itself and its potential, as it began its work on change.

3. Debunking myths. The Texas school support team initiative centers on the belief that just as every child can learn and achieve at high levels, every school can become a place where all children achieve at high levels. Yet we found that some educators had lost sight of their potential to make a powerful difference in the lives of children. They revealed their beliefs through statements such as "These children cannot be expected to achieve at such high levels because of their severe home situations," or "Given the language background of most of our students, we're not likely to ever reach the state's achievement goals."

Because educators from high-achieving Title I schools participated in the school support teams, they served as credible examples that it *is* possible to raise achievement in high-poverty urban and rural environments. In so doing, they helped school personnel rediscover their capacity for creating learning environments in which all children can succeed.

4. Exploring options. It's easy to think that the way we've always done things is the only way to get things done. Yet we know that if we continue to use the same instructional practices and the same organizational strategies, student achievement is unlikely to budge. One of the important contributions school support teams make is helping school personnel explore new options and make decisions that can lead to verifiable evidence of success.

In some cases, educators may be unaware of legitimate options for selecting innovative instructional materials, exploring instructional approaches that are engaging and challenging to diverse learners, organizing time and space for more in-depth or community-based learning, structuring the use of fiscal resources for maximum impact, or effectively responding to conflicts among various stakeholders. School support teams can offer new ideas, provide literature and materials, and create environments in which educators feel comfortable suggesting their ideas to their colleagues.

But the Texas school support team coordinators consistently agreed that support teams need to do more than give schools options to consider. One way that school support teams can build a school's capacity to explore alternatives for itself is to assist it in becoming a learning community. By modeling collaborative approaches to decision-making and helping schools create structures for individual and collective inquiry, support teams encourage schools to develop sustainable in-house approaches to professional development and to see themselves as the locus of control for initiating change.

In one school, the support team's work included helping the school develop a "plan to plan." School personnel created a structure for answering key questions they needed to address in their plan, such as: how the core planning group would find uninterrupted time to meet; how other educators and community members should be involved; what resources might facilitate their planning; and what timeline might help the school accomplish its goals.

5. Enhancing commitment. If school support teams do their jobs well, the schools receiving support will be strongly committed to a plan of action capable of increasing the academic success of all students. The Texas initiative is a reminder that school personnel must see the plan as workable, substantive, and reflective of their ideas. Each staff person must see the importance of her contribution to the successful implementation of the plan. Without such commitment, the support team's work will result in a disconnected process and one more plan to be filed away.

Substantial Potential

The Texas experience illustrates the substantial potential of school support teams to provide meaningful assistance to high-poverty schools. Site-based teams report that their confidence as change facilitators is growing, and many of them have generated numerous ideas for improving teaching and learning. Many of the schools that received assistance are actively pursuing promising schoolwide programs.

At the same time, the Texas experience also reveals that the work of providing genuine support is difficult. It would be easier to establish "support" systems that were, in essence, monitoring systems. The experience of the past 30 years, however, makes all too clear the limitations of such an approach.

Educators in high-poverty schools need and deserve real support to improve teaching and learning. School support teams help teachers and administrators in these schools build on the strengths of their students and communities; gain

access to a wealth of information about instructional, curricular, and organizational options; and develop their own realistic plan for improving teaching and learning. In these ways, school support teams are fulfilling the vital mission set forth by Congress.

References

Levin, H. M., and W. S. Hopfenberg. (January 1991). "Don't Remediate: Accelerate!" *Principal* 70: 11-13.

Moffett, C. (Winter 1996). "School Support Teams: Facilitating Success in High-Poverty Schools." *Professional Development Newsletter.* Va.: ASCD.

Public Law 103-382, Improving America's Schools Act, Section 1117c. 1994.

Saxl, E. R., M. B. Miles, and A. Leiberman. (1989). *Assisting Change in Education.* New York: Center for Policy Research; Seattle: University of Washington; and Alexandria, Va.: Association for Supervision and Curriculum Development.

Joseph F. Johnson Jr. is Director of School Improvement Initiatives at the Charles A. Dana Center at the University of Texas at Austin, 2613 Speedway, Austin, TX 78712. **Margery Ginsberg** is an education consultant who provides technical assistance for conceptualizing, coordinating, and training school support teams throughout Texas. She can be reached at (303) 530-4182 or at 6033 Jay Road, Boulder, CO 80301.

NEEDS ASSESSMENT STUDY GROUP DIALOGUE GUIDE

The following pages (123–145) have been selected to encourage reflection on creating meaningful needs assessments and to stimulate a discussion of what schools need to know about themselves in order to create meaningful reform initiatives.

Before you begin, please select a group facilitator, a notetaker, and a reporter who will share the dialogue group's findings with the large group.

1. Briefly familiarize yourselves with the materials.
2. Focus on the scenario activity in Figure 3.4 (p. 45), entitled Case Study for the Montrose Elementary School Support Team.
3. Read the scenario and note
   a. The kinds and sources of information that are embedded in the scenario and that can help a school better understand its strengths and needs. (For example, there is information on retention. The source of this information might be school or school district records on retention rates.)

      Example:

Kind of Information	Source of Information
Retention rate	*School or district retention records*

   b. Other kinds and/or sources of information that might help a school better understand its strengths and needs. (For example, a school might want to know how parents/families feel about their children's education. The source of information for this might be parent surveys or a focus group.)

Kind of Information	Source of Information
Parent/family attitudes about the school	*Surveys or focus groups*

   c. Recommendations for developing a comprehensive needs assessment that can help a school initiate reform in meaningful ways.

4. An alternative exercise includes reviewing Instructions for Cooperative Learning Exercise on Successful Texas Schoolwide Programs (Item 2, p. 123) and working collaboratively with your group to identify examples of success in your own school, as well as indicators or evidence of the effectiveness of each of your examples. This exercise will assist your group in identifying existing strengths and engaging in dialogue about ways to deepen or expand those strengths.

5. The Comprehensive Needs Assessment Puzzle (Item 6, p. 145) provides many examples of topics and tools that can be examined as part of a comprehensive needs assessment. Your group may wish to identify two to three ways in which this puzzle could be used to benefit a school's understanding of itself.

INSTRUCTIONS FOR COOPERATIVE LEARNING EXERCISE
ON SUCCESSFUL TEXAS SCHOOLWIDE PROGRAMS

1. Team members identify a theme or themes on which to become an "expert":
   - Theme 1: Focus on the Academic Success of Every Student
   - Theme 2: No Excuses
   - Theme 3: Experimentation
   - Theme 4: Inclusivity: Everyone Is Part of the Solution
   - Theme 5: Sense of Family
   - Theme 6: Collaboration and Trust
   - Theme 7: Passion for Learning and Growing

2. Each team member individually reads the introduction to the report "Successful Texas Schoolwide Programs: Research Study Results" (Item 3, p. 124), which includes:
   - Background (p. 127)
   - Findings (p. 128)

3. Next, each team member reads the section on his or her theme, and then reviews it, noting examples from his or her own school that correspond to the theme (Seven Common Characteristics of Successful Texas Schoolwide Programs, Item 4, pp. 137–143). For example, if a team member is reading the section that contains *Theme 1: Focus on the Academic Success of Every Student,* an example from his or her own school that corresponds to theme might be that "most teachers plan lessons that focus on the academic success of each and every student."

4. Finally, each team member considers indicators that provide evidence that the example he or she has selected is effective. For instance, if an example is that "most teachers plan lessons that focus on the academic success of each and every student," an indicator of success might be that "more students in every classroom appear to be consistently engaged in learning experiences."

5. When all team members have finished finding examples and indicators for their themes, the team shares its findings and engages in dialogue. Each team selects a reporter and a recorder to note: (a) three key issues the team discussed, (b) the team's ideas and priorities, and (c) recommendations for next steps on the Research Review (Item 5, p. 144).

SUCCESSFUL TEXAS SCHOOLWIDE PROGRAMS: RESEARCH STUDY RESULTS

**The Charles A. Dana Center
The University of Texas at Austin
2613 Speedway
Austin, Texas 78712
(512) 475-9708**

October 1996

Funding for this product was provided by a grant from the Texas Education Agency through Elementary and Secondary Education Act (ESEA) Title I funds, with additional funding support provided by Region VIII Comprehensive Regional Assistance Center: the STAR (Supporting Texas Academic Renewal) Center

Acknowledgments

This report was based on a study of the following 26 schools:

Adams Elementary School, Cleburne ISD, Ina Lee Roden, Principal

Apple Springs Elementary School, Apple Springs ISD, Leroy Spencer, Principal

Boys Ranch High School, Boys Ranch ISD, Larry White, Principal

T. A. Brown Elementary School, Austin ISD, Letitia Hinojosa, Principal

Kate Burgess Elementary School, Wichita Falls ISD, Gail Taylor, Principal

C. F. Carr Elementary School, Dallas ISD, Jean Dixon, Principal

Cisco Elementary School, Cisco ISD, Mary Schustereit, Principal

East Side Elementary School, San Felipe-Del Rio CISD, Roberto Zaragoza, Principal

El Magnet at Zavala Elementary School, Ector County CISD, Marilee Holmes, Principal

A. G. Hilliard Elementary School, North Forest ISD, Rufus Allen, Principal

Hueco Elementary School, Socorro ISD, Elfida Gutierrez, Principal

R. L. Isaacs Elementary School, Houston ISD, Leon Pettis, Principal

Lamar Elementary School, Corpus Christi ISD, Yvonne Duran, Principal

Los Fresnos Intermediate School, Los Fresnos CISD, Myrna Brogdon, Principal

Leo Marcell Elementary School, Mission CISD, Aurora Delgado, Principal

Nixon-Smiley Middle School, Nixon-Smiley CISD, Gary Tausch, Principal

Lucille Pearson Elementary School, Mission CISD, Mona Parras, Principal

L. R. Pietzsch Elementary School, Beaumont ISD, Shirley Bonton, Principal

Sagamore Hill Elementary School, Forth ISD, Sherry Breed, Principal

E. J. Scott Elementary, Houston ISD, Artice D. Hedgemon, Principal

Annie Sims Elementary School, Mount Pleasant ISD, Judy Walker, Principal

Springlake Junior High, Springlake-Earth ISD, Bill Verden, Principal

Sunrise Elementary School, Amarillo ISD, Richard Ross, Principal

Three Way School, Three Way ISD, Don Paris, Principal

West Avenue Elementary School, North East ISD, Jacqueline Lee, Principal

George C. Wolffarth Elementary School, Lubbock ISD, Armando Garcia, Principal

Each of the 26 schools allowed a team of researchers to visit their campus, conduct interviews, and make observations. The school personnel, parents, community members, and students generously gave of their time so that others could learn from their experiences. Without their passion for excellence and their willingness to share, this report would not exist. Special thanks to El Magnet at Zavala Elementary, Hueco Elementary, Los Fresnos Intermediate, Pietzsch Elementary, and Scott Elementary who allowed a team of researchers to return for a second, more extensive visit.

Primary Authors
Laura Lein, Ph.D.
Joseph F. Johnson, Jr., Ph.D.
Mary Ragland

Research Staff and Contributing Authors
Kim Anderson
Rose Asera, Ph.D.
Margery Ginsberg, Ph.D.
Veena Kaul
Liz Lilliott
Sandra Okolica
Janine Saunders
Darlene Yanez

The Charles A. Dana Center
The University of Texas at Austin
Philip Uri Treisman, Ph.D., Executive Director
Joseph F. Johnson, Jr., Ph.D., Director of School Improvement Initiatives
Rose Asera, Ph.D., Director of Research and Evaluation
Mary Ragland, Project Director

Background

Contrary to what is heard and read in mass media and educational literature, there is good reason to be hopeful about the education of students who attend public schools in poor communities. Schools where almost all students live in low-income situations can be schools in which almost all students achieve high levels of academic success. This is known not in theory, but in the practice and the results generated by real schools in Texas.

Through a grant provided by the Texas Education Agency and funding support from the U. S. Department of Education's Region VIII Comprehensive Center: the STAR Center (Support for Texas Academic Renewal), the Charles A. Dana Center at the University of Texas at Austin has studied schools in Texas that met all three of the following important criteria:

1. In the 1994–95 school year, the schools had a high percentage of students who met the federal criteria to receive free or reduced-price lunches. All of the schools had over 60 percent of the students meet free or reduced-price lunch criteria. Most of the schools had over 75 percent of the students meet the same criteria.

2. The schools received Title I funds and were at various stages of implementing Title I schoolwide programs (an approach involving the use of Title I funds to improve the entire school).

3. In the spring of 1995, in each school, at least 70 percent of the students passed the reading section of the Texas Assessment of Academic Skills (TAAS) and at least 70 percent of the students passed the mathematics section of the assessment. In 1995, few Texas schools had reached this level of academic achievement. The 70 percent criterion was selected because it was a key element for identifying schools as "recognized" in the state's accountability system.

In total, the criteria led to the identification of over 50 schools in Texas that were among those most heavily impacted by poverty, yet where achievement on the state's assessment of academic skills was among the highest of all schools in the state. Individually, each of the schools represents an existence proof that high-poverty schools can ensure high levels of academic success for almost all students. Furthermore, in combination, the schools suggest that there are good practices that would enable any high-poverty school to create an environment in which almost all students achieve high levels of academic success. The purpose of our study was to identify those key practices and to bring them to the attention of teachers, principals, parents, and other educational leaders.

Limited resources did not allow us to study all of the schools that met the three criteria. Thus, from the list of over 50 schools, 26 schools were selected to represent the diversity of Texas. As such, schools were selected from 18 of the state's 20 regional education service centers. The 26 schools included urban and rural schools, from large and small districts, and served very diverse ethnic populations.

Our team of researchers and educators spent the spring semester of 1996 visiting these schools and interviewing teachers, principals, parents, aides, support personnel, and central office administrators. We observed classrooms, playgrounds, lunch rooms, and staff meetings. We listened to the stories of their struggles, their successes, and their failures. We read their plans, pored over their data, and tried to understand the roots of their success. After visiting all of the schools once, we returned to conduct more in-depth visits at five of the schools.

Our approach relied heavily on qualitative, case study research methodology. Merriam (1988) explained that case study research designs are appropriate when description and explanation are sought (in contrast to prediction), when there are many variables within a case (as opposed to relatively few variables across many cases), and when a holistic picture of the case is desired (as opposed to a narrow picture with limited dimensions). Thus, case study methodology seemed appropriate for this project.

Merriam also explained that the nature of case study research allows for the evolution of questions throughout the research process. Sometimes, all of the right questions are not known prior to data collection activities. Sometimes, in the process of collecting data, new questions emerge. Thus, our team of researchers met frequently to compare notes and discuss findings. New hypotheses emerged as we visited schools and came to deeper understandings of the common characteristics among the schools. These common characteristics are described in the following section.

Findings

Before describing what we found, it is probably important to describe what was not found. First, if there is a magic formula, a simple prescription, or a miracle program that makes all the difference, we did not find it. We found more differences than similarities in the instructional programs and approaches used in the 26 schools. Some schools used whole language approaches, while others focused more on phonics. Some used constructivist learning approaches, while others engaged in direct teaching. Some were making cutting edge uses of instructional technology, while in others, computer technology was virtually absent in instruction. Some of the schools had joined Henry Levin's Accelerated Schools Project. Some were becoming engaged in the Success for All Program from Johns Hopkins University. Some were using Reading Recovery approaches. Others seemed to take pride in not having a clear allegiance to any specific program or methodology.

Also, it should be noted that although all of these schools achieved important accomplishments, the schools did not perceive themselves, nor did they wish to be perceived as perfect. They recognized their potential for further growth and they were committed to their ongoing improvement. In each area where we identified common characteris-

tics, a large percentage of the schools exemplified the characteristics, while a few of the 26 schools might not have been strong in that particular area. In other words, each of the schools had areas of strength, and each of the schools had areas where they might improve. Nonetheless, these schools have all achieved important and impressive results.

The common characteristics can be grouped into seven areas or themes. These themes describe the common attitudes, activities, and aspirations of the schools studied. The themes describe the attributes that have influenced the growth and success of the schools. The reader will quickly note that the themes are closely related and to some extent interdependent. Thus, in some ways the division of the themes seems artificial. However, the themes provide an easier way to discuss the complexities of the schools studied.

Theme 1: *Focus on the Academic Success of Every Student*

Many studies of effective schools emphasized the extent to which successful schools shared a common mission (Texas Education Agency 1989). Similarly, a study of 12 successful Title I schoolwide projects (U. S. Department of Education 1994) found that the schools had an agreed-upon vision for all students that was based on higher academic standards. Our study underscores these findings. In all of the 26 schools studied, there was a strong focus on the academic success of every student.

It should be noted that these schools did not simply have a mission. Rather, they had the mission of ensuring the academic success of every student. They did not merely have mission statements. Their sense of mission was articulated in every aspect of their planning, organization, and use of resources.

Almost every decision about the selection of instructional materials or strategies; the adoption of staff development strategies; the use of fiscal resources; the scheduling of the school calendar; the assignment and use of teachers, support personnel, and volunteers; the use of classroom, playground, and building space; or the use of any other resources was guided by a focus on the mission of ensuring the academic success of every student. For example, when the staff at one school decided to supplement the district's whole-language curriculum with phonics-based instruction, it was because they had reason to believe that such a change would allow them to improve the reading achievement of more students. When the staff at another school decided to seek a modification of their school's instructional week, it was done with the goal of creating more time for teachers to come together to plan and learn more about improving instruction.

As mentioned earlier, these schools used a great variety of instructional approaches. However, common among the schools is that they chose their approaches because they believed that the particular approach would be effective in meeting the specific needs of their students and in utilizing the unique strengths of their staff and community. Their beliefs about various approaches were influenced strongly by their formal and informal efforts to collect and analyze information that helped them determine which policies, programs, and practices were most likely to result in improved academic achievement for their students.

"What's best for kids?" was heard repeatedly in the 26 schools as a benchmark for making decisions. To determine what was best, some teachers developed small, informal pilot studies to empirically determine the approaches that were most likely to lead to the academic success of their students. In other cases, educators reviewed the educational literature related to their area of concern and came to conclusions about what might work best with their students. In some cases, principals and teachers visited other schools within or outside of Texas to learn about promising practices. They asked challenging questions to determine the potential of those practices to influence the academic success of their students.

The focus on the academic success of every student was evident in the planning of individual teachers, just as it was evident in whole school planning activities. Teachers planned lessons with a focus on getting each and every student to succeed academically. Teachers were attuned to the special ways in which individual students learned best. They exploited this knowledge to create learning environments that allowed many students to attain challenging academic skills.

In almost all of the 26 schools, teachers were supported in their planning through extensive school and/or district efforts to align curriculum, staff development, and technology purchases with the objectives of the TAAS. Teachers were more likely to use teacher guides as tools for accomplishing instructional objectives rather than as scripts that they were required to follow. Teachers knew what objective they were teaching and why the particular instructional approach was most likely to work with their students.

Formative assessment results were used widely by teachers to assist them in planning instruction. In some schools, teachers used their own formative assessments; in other schools, teachers used formative assessments created by the school district. In either case, the formative assessments allowed teachers to accurately determine areas of strength and need. When students had mastered the expected skills, teachers frequently went further into other extensions and applications of the academic skills.

Teachers consistently reported that they were actively supported by their principals as they attempted to focus on the academic success of every student. "She'll get us whatever we need" was articulated by many teachers in many schools as they spoke of their principals. Teachers felt supported with adequate instructional materials and relevant staff development. Similarly, principals often indicated that they felt supported by their superintendents and central office colleagues. As well, there was often strong support from the community through volunteer activities and school/business partnerships. As such, the mission seemed to be shared by everyone. There seemed to be little doubt that a school would be successful in improving achievement because everyone (including teachers, support staff, parents, central office staff, and community leaders) had a role in actualizing the school's mission.

Theme 2: *No Excuses*

Even when schools have a strong sense of mission, there are times when the mission is not achieved, when students do not learn as much or do not perform as well as expected. In such situations, the tendency might be to blame or to make excuses; however, the schools we studied did not accept excuses for failure with any student. Educators at these schools tended to believe that they could succeed with any student, regardless of the nature of the home situation, regardless of the student's previous performance or diagnosis, regardless of resource difficulties, and regardless of whatever other constraints might confront the school. Ultimately, there were no excuses for low performance.

In almost all of the 26 schools, teachers talked about students who lived in difficult situations (often related to their families' low income). However, the teachers never accepted that the difficult situation was a reason to lower their academic expectations for students. Instead the teachers often engaged in creative efforts to respond to the situation. Whether it meant having the student do his homework after school each day, calling home to provide a wake-up call on mornings when the mother worked the night shift, allowing a student to take extra portions of lunch home in the afternoon so that she would have dinner, or modeling to a mother how to read a story to her preschool child, the school personnel evidenced a powerful "whatever it takes" attitude.

In several schools educators commented, "Money is not going to keep any child from participating." Schools were creative in finding ways to stretch their Title I budgets, to use their parent-teacher organizations to raise funds, to tie into existing community services, or to broker new

support from business partners. In some cases, school personnel went as far as to use their own personal financial resources to assist students with basic needs such as food and clothing.

Similarly, a lack of resources was not accepted as an excuse for providing any less than an excellent academic program. When funds were needed for professional development activities, instructional technology, or other instructional materials, educators demonstrated both persistence and creativity in "finding" the needed funds. Some schools sought new funding from state, federal, or private grant sources. Others developed new business partnerships. In many cases, schools became very deliberate in prioritizing the use of their discretionary resources, including their Title I dollars. They made tough choices and eliminated less effective expenditures so that they could afford expenditures that would more likely result in greater student achievement.

For schools in general, rules and regulations present a different type of barrier that can sometimes impede a school's ability to respond to the unique situations of students. While some schools might accept such barriers as legitimate excuses for failure, many of the schools we studied took a dramatically different approach. In essence, these educators seemed to assume that rules must be negotiable if they impair the school's ability to meet the needs of students. Principals were willing to debate with the food services director, the city fire marshal, the transportation director, or whoever seemed to be imposing a rule that did not seem to serve students well. Often, their persuasiveness and persistence were rewarded with compromises, waivers, or other efforts to relax requirements.

In schools where the motivation to achieve was so strong, one might have expected to see more blaming when results did not meet expectations; however, educators at the schools we studied did not blame their students, parents, outside forces, or each other. Instead, they reflected upon their own efforts to find opportunities to improve. Also, we saw schools celebrating their accomplishments and acknowledging the contributions of the teachers, support personnel, parents, students, and administrators who had a role in the success. At the same time, we saw thoughtful consideration of the steps that needed to be taken to build upon prior successes toward the goal of high achievement for all students.

Several effective schools studies have focused on the importance of high expectations (Texas Education Agency 1989). The schools we studied definitely evidenced high expectations for their students; however, they also evidenced high expectations for themselves. The school personnel knew that their students would achieve impressive results because they knew that they, as a school staff, would take whatever steps were necessary to ensure each student's success. Repeatedly, school staff evidenced a willingness to work diligently for long hours, often beyond the requests of their supervisors. Educators defined their jobs based on what needed to be done to reach challenging goals, not by traditional job descriptions and not by traditional notions of work days or work weeks.

Theme 3: *Experimentation*

Closely related to the "no excuses" theme, we found the 26 schools to be places where careful experimentation was encouraged. Educators felt such strong responsibility for ensuring the academic success of students that they eagerly sought ways to improve teaching and learning. If an approach was not working with one student or any group of students, teachers were allowed, encouraged, and even expected to try different approaches. Thus, experimentation flourished as individual teachers, grade-level teams, site-based decision-making teams, and entire school staffs considered new ways to stimulate the achievement of students.

Educators were very careful in their choice of experiments. They evidenced a great sense of responsibility for selecting courses of action that had a high likelihood of leading to improved student performance. Nonetheless, when experiments did not lead to the desired result, we did not see reprisals or negative consequences. Instead, educators were expected to use the failure experience as part of the improvement process. Teachers and other school staff had the opportunity to make a good try, fail, learn from the experience, and make modifications or refinements that led to improved results. Thus, educators often exuded optimism about eventually getting every student to attain the highest standards of performance.

Experimentation was evident at many levels. Schools often engaged in pilot tests of materials or strategies before considering adoptions by the entire school. Schools experimented with the organization of the school day, the acquisition and use of technology, the use of intersessions, and the assignment of support staff. Teachers often shared and cooperated in each other's experiments and dialogued about their findings. They learned from each other's successes and failures.

As teachers and administrators engaged in experimentation, they also encouraged students to experiment and identify new ways to accomplish tasks. Teachers often helped students feel that it was acceptable to try new ideas and approaches. If the approach failed, school personnel were there to assist the student in refining the approach. Thus, students were taught that failure is just a step that sometimes precedes success.

Theme 4: *Inclusivity: Everyone Is Part of the Solution*

In the schools we studied, it seemed that everyone who might possibly come in contact with a student was a partner in ensuring that student's academic success. Job titles did not matter as much as one's potential to contribute. Thus, teachers at all grade levels in both regular and special programs, professional support personnel such as nurses and counselors, bus drivers, campus administrators, custodians, school office staff, cafeteria workers, instructional aides, librarians, parent volunteers, part-time personnel, community leaders, and students were often enlisted to be a part of the team that would lead a student to success at school. As such, everyone who worked at the school, attended the school, or sent children to attend the school had a strong sense of ownership.

Beyond their traditional designated roles, school personnel had broader roles as members of the school team. It was not unusual to see secretaries listening to students read, special education teachers problem-solving instructional strategies with grade-level teams of general classroom teachers, or librarians supporting parental involvement initiatives. The broadly defined roles allowed many individuals to assume leadership roles. In several schools, everyone on the staff was part of at least one committee and most of the staff chaired a committee at some time during the year.

Effective schools studies (Texas Education Agency 1989) and schoolwide program studies (Schenck and Beckstrom 1993, U. S. Department of Education 1994) have placed considerable focus on the importance of parental involvement. At the schools we visited, school personnel did not wait passively for parents to become involved in various aspects of the school. In almost all of the schools there was a multi-faceted outreach to families that constantly encouraged and supported parents in ways that nurtured greater involvement in their children's education. Educators made special efforts to make parents feel welcome. Open-door policies and open-door attitudes were common. School personnel assumed responsibility for creating an environment in which parents wanted to become involved.

Often, in these schools, students were utilized as important resources for improving their own and each other's academic achievement. Students had important roles in directing their learning experiences and had input into a variety of decisions that influenced their school experience. Additionally, students often were involved in cooperative learning or peer tutoring strategies in which they worked together to facilitate their learning.

Theme 5: *Sense of Family*

Beyond the inclusivity evidenced by the schools we studied, we observed a powerful sense of family. Not only were students, parents, and all school personnel included as a part of the team, they were also included as part of the school family. Overwhelmingly, the most common metaphor we observed in the schools was the school as a family. Statements such as "We're a family here" or "These are all my children" were heard frequently. Moreover, the actions of teachers, principals, students, parents, and other members of the school community frequently reflected the concern, dedication, involvement, respect, and love that one would expect to find in the healthiest of families. The school personnel saw the school less as an institution and more as a family.

In the schools we visited, students were treated with respect and concern. Teachers were concerned with the child's total development, not simply with student performance on the TAAS. As such, we saw considerable attention to areas of endeavor beyond the traditional academics, in areas such as music, art, or physical education. Similarly, attention was given to the social and emotional needs of students. Counselors, nurses, social workers, and family liaisons often took leadership roles in ensuring that students' basic needs were met. Traditional school roles were often blurred because educators were willing to do whatever was needed to ensure that their students were doing well physically, emotionally, and socially.

In many ways, the schools strove to communicate to students that they were valued individually and collectively. School activities, bulletin boards, and curriculum materials reflected and celebrated the cultural and linguistic diversity of the students. Similarly, hallways, classrooms, doors, and ceilings were often used to display student work. School personnel often created opportunities to recognize the academic and nonacademic accomplishments of students. Students did not need to misbehave to get attention because school staff were engaged in so many efforts to attend to the positive contributions of students.

Students were treated with respect and courtesy. Like family, the school provided a safe place for students to grow and learn responsibility. School personnel were able to empathize with students and relate to their personal experiences. In many of the schools, teachers and other staff grew up in the same neighborhoods and had similar backgrounds. Adults at the schools acted in ways that showed that they were happy that the students were there. When disciplinary issues arose (which generally seemed rare), the issues were handled consistently, quickly, fairly, and in a manner that still demonstrated respect for the individual student. Although consistent, school personnel still recognized that there were situations when the rules did not seem appropriate. In such cases, school personnel chose to sacrifice consistency for the sake of a child, instead of the opposite.

Also, respect for students was reflected in a tendency to avoid or minimize the use of labels. When teachers grouped students, they were careful to avoid stigmatizing students. Thus, groupings were often heterogeneous or they were sufficiently fluid to avoid labeling. Special programs were often located or organized in ways that minimized the separation or stigmatization of students.

Just as students were treated as valued members of the school family, so were their parents. In many of the schools, parents were provided a special place to help make them comfortable when they came to school. To help make sure that parents felt at home, office staff, principals, teachers, and other school personnel greeted parents warmly, usually by name. Parents at these schools knew they were welcome; they knew that they belonged as part of the school family.

It is hard to feel like a family member if you cannot understand the language. Therefore, school personnel made many efforts to accommodate parents who did not speak English. Bilingual office staff, the frequent use of interpreters, bilingual signs and banners throughout the school, and bilingual newsletters were among the strategies used to help parents feel comfortable at school, even when they could not speak English. Similarly, the tone and words used to communicate with parents was often one that reflected respect for the parents' language, dialect, and background. Teachers did not expect parents to understand educational jargon nor did they talk to parents in ways that were condescending.

Even when parents were having difficulty assuming traditional parenting roles, school personnel responded in ways that demonstrated their respect for the challenging situations parents faced. Teachers seemed to be able to empathize with the difficulties faced by some parents, and supported parents as they worked to improve their involvement in their child's academic life. School personnel focused more on seeking solutions than on blaming parents for the academic or social difficulties that students encountered.

The sense of family extended beyond students and parents to all members of the school staff. At the schools we studied, all school personnel, regardless of position or tenure, were perceived as important members of the school family. New teachers were valued for their fresh ideas and perspectives. Veteran teachers were valued for their experience and expertise. The importance of each staff member was based in part on his or her contribution to the mission of the school, but moreover, their importance was based on their worth as an individual. Staff members cared about each other's lives beyond the school, in addition to caring about their performance at the school.

Often principals took a lead role in finding a variety of ways to let school personnel know that they were appreciated and respected. School personnel were acknowledged for their accomplishments, their expertise, and just for their membership as part of the school family. Each of the schools found ways to utilize both the personal and professional strengths of staff members, often beyond their traditional job descriptions.

As in any family, there were concerns, hurt feelings, and disagreements; however, the areas of disagreement were usually much smaller than the areas of agreement. When there were hurt feelings, people were quick to respond in ways that re-affirmed the value of the individual to the entire school family.

One of the characteristics that make these schools seem more like big families is the absence of an "us" versus "them" attitude. All of the members of the school family worked to support each other. There was a powerful sense of belonging evidenced by students, parents, teachers, support personnel, and administrators. The school family was a support network that included many smaller support networks. The strong support of the networks enabled many students, teachers, parents, and other school staff to transcend difficult situations and achieve impressive successes.

Theme 6: *Collaboration and Trust*

Whereas theme four focused on the ways in which students, families, and school personnel were considered part of the team that would accomplish the school's mission, and theme five focused on the ways in which students, families, and school personnel were treated as valued members of the school family, this next theme focuses primarily on the way in which school personnel worked and learned together. Clearly, there is overlap because both the emphasis on inclusion and the sense of family influence the way school personnel work together. Nonetheless, the ways in which educators were working together, in cooperation and trust, seemed to substantially influence their success.

The importance of collaboration was empha-sized in other studies of effective schoolwide pro-grams (U.S. Department of Education 1994). In the schools we studied, openness, honesty, and trust characterized most of the interactions among school personnel. School personnel openly shared con-

cerns and successes with each other. They provided assistance to each other and learned from each other. Teachers seemed to prefer working in teams and did so frequently. Team teaching arrangements were used often. Thus, when problems arose, school staff generally did not need to respond alone. They had colleagues who helped discuss issues and provide ideas, feedback, and encouragement.

Although there was collaboration, there was also disagreement. Teachers and other school personnel frequently reported that they felt free to express their concerns about ideas or actions, without fear of reprisal. There were opportunities for staff to disagree and work out their disagreements in constructive manners. Although the schools typically acted as teams, they still respected each individual's right to disagree.

The openness of the collaborations allowed many teachers to feel comfortable sharing their areas of weakness. Often, teams of teachers helped compensate for each others' weaknesses. Teachers frequently explained partnerships that started with statements such as, "If you can help me with my math lessons, I'll help you with social studies."

Cooperation at these schools extended beyond their grade-span groupings. Frequently, teachers worked with those who taught subsequent grade levels to improve their understanding of each other's curricula and expectations. Even when the next grade level was at a different school, teachers often assumed responsibility for reaching out and estab-lishing the collaborative relationships that would allow them to better ensure their students' future success.

Administrators at these schools made sure that teachers and other school personnel had many opportunities to collaborate and work together. There were many formal and informal forums that provided school personnel with opportunities to openly discuss programs and policies. School personnel were encouraged to express their con-cerns freely, without fear of reprisal. Similarly, administrators often took responsibility for ensuring that teachers had the time to meet and plan together. Often school personnel credited administrators for setting the tone that helped the school become a place where staff worked well together toward common goals.

Theme 7: *Passion for Learning and Growing*

What happens when a teacher sets a challenging goal for a group of students and the students achieve the goal? What happens when the entire school establishes a difficult goal and achieves it? At the schools we visited, many lofty goals had been set and attained. Yet, we did not see people "resting on their laurels." We did not see people becoming complacent with their current ways of teaching, organizing, or leading. Although schools clearly took time to celebrate their successes, there was almost an immediate redefinition of higher goals. School staff continued to challenge and push themselves toward the attainment of even higher goals. Teachers sometimes expressed concerns about ceiling effects and similar measurement phenomena, but the "no excuses" attitude discussed in Theme 2 generally prevailed. Despite those concerns, school personnel continued working to improve teaching and learning.

The experimentation discussed in Theme 3 did not stop when the desired results were attained. Instead school staff focused on how they could improve upon strategies or identify new strategies that would allow them to succeed with even more students or that would allow them to take students to even higher levels of success. In these schools there is a continuous seeking after new horizons, new opportunities, new ways of operating. The process of such discovery and learning on the part of all participants is considered the central business of the school.

Planning for improvement is perpetual. At the schools we visited, there is an unyielding belief that improvement is possible. The pressure to improve was almost totally self-imposed. Yet, these schools were more focused on improving their performance than some schools with dramatically less success. We describe this phenomenon as a passion for growing and learning.

To actualize their improvement plans, school personnel were almost always engaged in learning activities. Professional development was not an event at these schools: it was part of the culture, part of the way of life. In the schools we studied, we frequently found school personnel engaged in extensive efforts to bring new information into the school. Federal, state, and local resources were used to send staff to attend conferences, to visit highly effective schools, and to critically observe promising programs. At the same time, teachers and other personnel shared journal articles and discussed educational literature that enriched their discussions about how to improve.

The frequent analysis of data (as discussed in Theme 1) allowed teachers to learn from their own practice, and the regular collaborations (as discussed in Theme 6) often led school personnel to adopt approaches that built upon the successes of individual teachers or groups of teachers. Thus, teachers and other school personnel were often learning as much about teaching as their students were learning about reading, mathematics, and other areas of the school curriculum.

It was easy to see how the educators' passion for learning and growing had been transmitted to students. Students exhibited both confidence in their ability to improve and eagerness to grow intellectually. Similarly, parents were often engaged in learning activities. In most of the schools, parents participated in formal and informal efforts to improve their capacity to assist the school in ensuring their child's academic success. Thus, the inclusivity described in Theme 4 is an important element in the passion for learning and growing.

These schools can truly be characterized as communities of learners. As school personnel learned and grew, so did parents, and so did students. Learning, growing, and improving were the focus of thousands of interactions among students, parents, and school personnel. Nonetheless, these schools did not fail to remember that every participant in the community of learners was first an individual, an important and valued member of the school family. This constant reaffirmation, support, and validation (as described in Theme 5) was probably responsible for individuals finding the strength to confront daunting barriers, overcome those barriers, achieve impressive goals, and then refocus their sights on even higher goals for student performance.

Bibliography

Merriam, S. B. (1988) *Case Study Research in Education: A Qualitative Approach*. San Francisco, CA: Jossey-Bass.

Schenck, E. A., & Beckstrom, S. (1993) *Chapter 1 Schoolwide Project Study*. Portsmouth, NH: RMC Research Corporation.

Texas Education Agency. (1989) *Effective Schools Research and Dropout Reduction*. Austin, Texas: Author.

U.S. Department of Education. (1994) *An Idea Book: Implementing Schoolwide Projects*. Washington, DC: Author.

SEVEN COMMON CHARACTERISTICS OF SUCCESSFUL TEXAS SCHOOLWIDE PROGRAMS

Theme 1: Focus on the Academic Success of Every Student

Examples	Indicators
e.g.: The mission of the school is to ensure the academic success of every student.	e.g.: Teachers are shaping their practice to support the special ways in which individual students learn best. Lesson plans regularly feature opportunities for students to create projects to demonstrate learning.

Theme 2: No Excuses

Examples	Indicators
e.g.: Teachers have agreed to have a "no-blame" policy toward parents and one another in order to enhance their sense of personal responsibility for the success of each child.	e.g.: There is increased parent involvement as teachers work more closely with parents to reach less engaged students.

Theme 3: Experimentation

Examples	Indicators
e.g.: Teachers are trying to use technology in more innovative ways in their classrooms.	e.g.: Teachers believe that their heightened responsibility for learning to effectively use technology is influencing students' enthusiasm for learning. More students appear to be actively involved in learning.

Theme 4: Inclusivity: Everyone Is Part of the Solution

Examples	Indicators
e.g.: Everyone on staff—including secretaries and custodians—is a mentor to at least one student.	e.g.: Attendance has significantly improved among low achieving students. Personal attention also appears to be influencing motivation to learn. Students who are reading with their mentors are reading more in class.

Theme 5: Sense of Family

Examples	Indicators
e.g.: Staff members care about one another's lives beyond the school, in addition to caring about their performance at school.	e.g.: Absenteeism among new and more experienced teachers is low.

Theme 6: Collaboration and Trust

Examples	Indicators
e.g.: Administrators support teachers in expressing their ideas and concerns freely without fear of reprisal.	e.g.: Active participation and a can-do spirit at staff meetings provide evidence that the school community is working together to solve emerging challenges.

Theme 7: Passion for Learning and Growing

Examples	Indicators
e.g.: Planning for improvement is perpetual. The entire staff revisits the schoolwide plan on a quarterly basis to assess progress and make adjustments.	e.g.: Teachers consistently express their belief that they are a community of learners and they are learning as much about teaching as their students are learning about reading, mathematics, and other aspects of the school curriculum.

RESEARCH REVIEW

Key Issues That We Identified/Discussed	New Ideas/Priorities	Recommendations for Next Steps Related to This Research	Questions/Comments

COMPREHENSIVE NEEDS ASSESSMENT

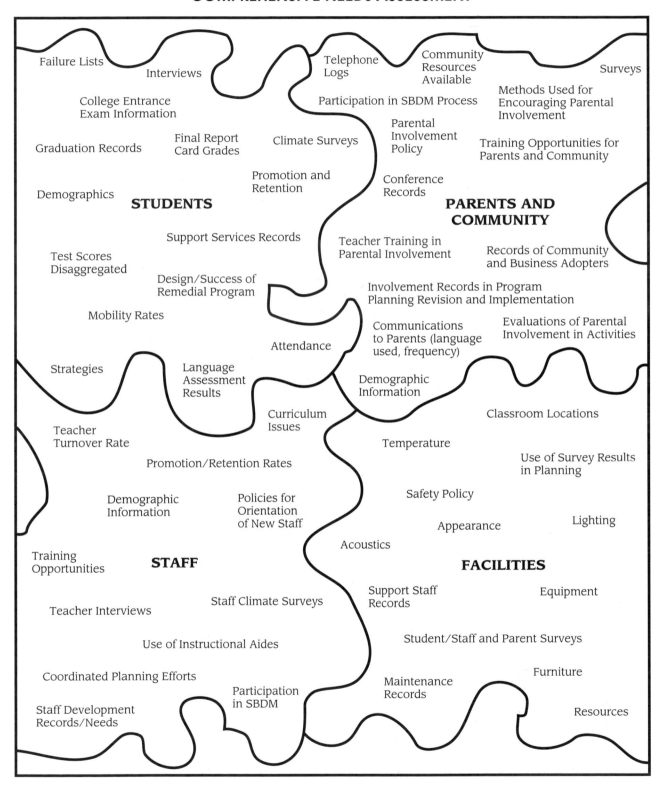

—Contributed by Pat Roland, Region XVI Education Service Center, Amarillo, Texas.

Site-Based Facilitation of Empowered Schools: Complexities and Issues for Staff Developers

Carl D. Glickman
Richard Hayes
Frances Hensley

The complexities of promoting school change can be minimized through the effective use of facilitators.

Carl D. Glickman is executive director, Program for School Improvement and professor, Department of Educational Leadership, University of Georgia, Aderhold Hall, Athens, GA 30802. Richard Hayes is an associate, Program for School Improvement and professor, Department of Counseling Education, University of Georgia. Frances Hensley is an associate, Program for School Improvement and assistant professor, Department of Instructional Technology, University of Georgia.

The League of Professional Schools, begun in the 1989-90 school year, is a network of 43 elementary, middle, and secondary public schools throughout Georgia who meet regularly with each other and the staff of the University of Georgia's Program for School Improvement to sustain school renewal in shared governance, school-wide instructional innovations, and school-based action research. Empowerment and site-based decision making have been used to promote such change. The League has received national recognition (silver medalist award from the Business-Higher Education Forum in 1991 and 1992) and validation as an exemplary program (recognized by the National Diffusion Network in 1991) for positive educational changes in schools as they restructure themselves. Based on our experiences with League schools, we have identified a number of complexities in the school change process. We also have determined a number of ways that staff developers could be helpful in addressing these complexities.

The League of Professional Schools defines empowerment as teachers having a majority voice in school educational decisions (staff development; curriculum; in-structional innovations; reorganization of teaching time, grouping, and staffing; assessments of learning) with the principal having the same right and influence as any individual faculty member without a veto over the decisions of the group. League schools operate with a variety of decision-making rules, including consensus, two-thirds, and majority vote.

Over the past years, league members have learned more about the critical role of school facilitation. In the first year of school change, approximately 20% of League schools needed little help--they were "naturals" with already existing internal working relationships of trust and collegiality. Another 60% of League schools have needed quarterly re-focusing sessions and an occasional visit from an outsider to keep them on track. The other 20% of the schools have required intensive facilitation.

The League of Professional Schools includes only schools where teachers and principals *voluntarily* tackle shared decision-making, improved instruction, and school-based action research. We speculate that in districts where schools are *mandated* to have shared governance, the percentages of schools needing intensive, external facilita-

146

tion would be considerably higher than the League's 20%.

To expect schools to successfully work in a collegial manner without prior planning, staff development, and facilitation assistance is generally unrealistic. Indeed, most schools will need help--particularly in the early stages--because the work of empowerment, governance, restructuring, and most importantly, improving education for students is complicated and, at times, painful.

Complexities of School Change

Through our experiences with League schools, we have found six complexities of school change. We have also discovered that schools can overcome the following complexities with the assistance of skilled facilitation.

Complexity 1: Conflict will increase. Groups that are involved in designing ingenious ways of solving problems can expect more conflict than they experienced when decisions were made by hierarchical authorities (Johnson & Johnson, 1987). As group members come to know themselves and one another better, especially within the context of the evolving group, confrontation and conflict inevitably arise (Tuckman & Jensen, 1977). Because conflict is a part of the change process when members take their shared governance responsibilities seriously, conflict should not be avoided but rather be encouraged.

In empowerment efforts, dormant or suppressed differences in opinion rise to the surface. For example, one elementary school found a rather innocuous concern about improving discipline sparking debate about administrative responsibilities, teaching effectiveness, multicultural sensitivity, and family support. It was only through the airing of such diverse and heated perspectives that the faculty was able to understand the need for involving many people in an effort to make appropriate decisions.

An ideological debate such as the one just described creates a wider arena of knowledge (Ward, 1989), gives the group a clearer picture of implementation obstacles, and encourages people to express their ideas and opinions more openly and honestly. A facilitator can help group members understand the value of such conflict and mediate it in a way that protects individuals from being personally diminished while at the same time elevating the debate into critical inquiry

(Hayes, In press). In the prior examples, faculty and administrators argued with each other, but at most (if not, all) times, a facilitator helped keep the debate focused on the issues rather than on the personalities involved.

Complexity 2: Assessment information will cultivate critical dissatisfaction. As a school attempts to establish educational priorities, it may tend to use the cardiac approach to assessment--"in our hearts, we're doing fine" (Wolfe, 1969). Such subjective data tend to reinforce the idea that if student learning and attitudes aren't quite what they should be, the locus of responsibility rests with students, parents, community, or the school board, but not with the professional staff.

The facilitator needs to encourage members to examine these basic assumptions (Bion, 1959) and to test their efficacy in the real world of the school. To ensure that group members have assessment information beyond their own perceptions, the facilitator can help each group develop and analyze appropriate measures such as student and parent surveys, structured interviews, classroom observations, test scores, promotion rates, discipline referrals, placement in special classes, and new learning assessments.

To prevent possible perpetuation of inequities, such data should be compared by student race, socio-economic class, and gender. For example, a highly regarded high school was urged to go beyond certain highly publicized data (student honors, admission into highly selective colleges, SAT scores, achievement tests) and to examine the data more closely. It turned out that only a quarter of the students accounted for the school's high regard. Other than that group of students, the school appeared quite ordinary. The staff was defensive about the information ("What do you expect us to be--all things for all people?").

The facilitator was able to redirect the group's thinking by asking "If you were to maintain the achievement you currently have but do only one or two things to improve achievement for the rest of the students, what would you do?" From that question came suggestions and the eventual development of a transition program for ninth graders and a rearrangement of academic extracurriculum activities to provide greater access to all students.

In their classic studies on effective

schools, Brookover, Beady, Flood, Schweiter, and Wisenbaker (1979) found that faculty in improving schools were more dissatisfied with their instruction than faculty in schools where little improvement occurs. Thus, group facilitators should help group members accept such data as helpful feedback rather than as a threat to their past actions. Comprehensive data, beyond subjective feelings, helps cultivate a critical and sensitive look at teaching and learning in the school.

Complexity 3: Without new information, decisions will be made that reinforce the status quo. Related to item number two, a facilitator needs to help the group make implementation decisions based upon current information. Without such information, a faculty may feel justified in continuing a present practice or reinstituting a former practice.

Most schools will need help--particularly in the early stages--because the work of empowerment, governance, restructuring, and most importantly, improving education for students is complicated and, at times, painful.

For example, a middle school was stuck. Every time the issue of lack of student motivation came up, the school had gone to contracting (and "getting tough") with parents and caretakers to see that homework was done, attendance was punctual, and students paid attention. The results hadn't been promising but the same solutions were used again and again. Only after the facilitator suggested the need to canvas the literature and visit other schools working on the same concern did the faculty start to question their own teaching techniques as being too passive and not applicable to students interests outside of school.

Without new information, decisions will be made with only participants' existing knowledge base. Restructuring schools without knowledge of innovative approaches is likely to result in the same struc-

Faculty in improving schools were more dissatisfied with their instruction than faculty in schools where little improvement occurs.

tures as before. In fact, school personnel may be reluctant to seek new information that could mean revisions of programs which they complain about but are comfortable in using.

Again, facilitators can help group members examine their own motives and assumptions relative to any proposed change and to bring new insights to their decisions through exposure to the latest research, relevant journal articles, case studies, visits to other schools, and consultation with recognized experts in areas of interest.

The building of an expanded knowledge base is essential to finding new answers. Whether it be improving achievement, reducing the dropout rate, or increasing cooperative behaviors, a school needs information beyond what it currently possesses.

Complexity 4: With immediate school success, pressure for more short-term success will increase at the potential cost of long-term student gains. Many first-year school empowerment efforts result in some immediate improvements such as increases in faculty morale, improvement of student attitudes, rises in achievement test scores, and revisions of some curricula. With such public success, schools often become concerned about whether next year's efforts will

The push for short-term gains can make a school deal with symptoms and superficial cures, but a more critical stance can help a school deal with causes and more lasting solutions.

show similar immediate results. In the face of such optimism, facilitators should assist groups in reflecting upon and attending to more "strategic" plans for school improvement priorities and issues (Pfeiffer, Goodstein, & Nolan, 1989).

Because production and factory metaphors are so often used in schools, the mentality of "more goals, faster success" can come at the expense of a more lasting mission of "fewer goals, greater significance." Many faculty need help in identifying and thinking through this predicament.

For example, one League school found that it was relatively easy to improve student attendance with quick policy changes about enforcement, but the change did not address the underlying cause of apathy in the school or how to involve students meaningfully in their school. Initiatives to deal with these underlying causes would take two to five years.

Thus, the push for short-term gains can make a school deal with symptoms and superficial cures, but a more critical stance can help a school deal with causes and more lasting solutions. It is difficult, however, not to be enticed by quick answers that show ready, if not lasting, results. Balancing these immediate needs to show success with less immediate but more enduring improvements is an issue that a group facilitator needs to help members understand and address.

Complexity 5: Decisions about dreams will be easier to make than decisions about how to attain one's dreams. Empowered schools have an opportunity to rethink the conventions of the school. Curriculum, scheduling, grouping, and grading are all potential topics for discussion (Glickman, 1987). Dealing with "what if" questions can be stimulating and, at times, exhilarating. Such thinking, however, does not necessarily result in change. Indeed, once becoming comfortable with intellectual conflict, groups often spend their time in speculative and abstract areas, thereby making the group safe but unchanging.

Unless the group facilitator confronts members to think through proposed actions and their consequences, group members are likely to continue intellectual discourse and debate as a defense against making actual changes. Reid (1987) noted that those within an organization often complain about what exists and know what can be done, but they do not act. This reluctance arises be-

cause the old system, as dysfunctional as it might be, still feels safe and secure.

From a group facilitation perspective, it is important to help members acknowledge their insecurities about proposed changes and use this discomfort to develop plans for implementing the change (Yalom, 1985). Hall and Hord (1987) found that initial concerns with educational innovations or change are usually expressed as: "How will this innovation affect me personally? How will my life be changed?" Dealing directly with such questions helps members plan gradual steps to implement the dream.

Complexity 6: Criticism will develop from the outside. Empowered schools operate according to democratic principles and often find themselves criticized by other schools. As an empowered school attains success and recognition for efforts on behalf of students, criticism from other educators often mounts. A facilitator is needed to help group members analyze the source and significance of such criticism and determine appropriate responses.

Although empowerment is an old concept (Dewey, 1916), there are relatively few schools that actually involve teachers as equals in educational decisions. Schools where the principal shares power but does not hold an absolute veto over school-wide educational matters are not common. This unconventional way of working earns a school the label as a "maverick," and most mavericks serve as lightening rods for both praise and hostility.

The hostility comes from three sources. One source of criticism is from schools that are exerting equivalent efforts but are not being recognized for their work. A second source is from schools which believe that public recognition is increasing pressure on them to act in a similar manner. As a school and as individuals, they might not be ready for or believe in such actions. By criticizing the innovative school, it deflects attention away from the conventional school. A third source of criticism is from schools or individual educators who believe that the recognition accorded to an empowered school is exaggerated and, at least partially, not deserved. Such critics suggest that, aside from the hyperbole, the empowered school is far removed from utopia.

To illustrate, an elementary school in a large district found itself in the center of a storm after making decisions over three years to reorganize grouping, scheduling,

148

and teaching activities. As a result, achievement measures were the highest in the district. Parents were highly satisfied, newspaper stories were written, and faculty and administrators were asked to speak throughout the state and nation.

Yet, the school found itself being ostracized in its own district and being left out of district policy discussions and pilot programs. Facilitators helped the school identify the sources of concern, and several discussions ensued with district personnel and other schools in the district. The school then made a conscious effort to speak publicly about its problems rather than its successes and to convey the message that it was not suggesting that its work should be every schools "cup of tea."

Facilitators need to help group members locate the source and rationale for different types of criticism and to keep members from adopting a reactive stance. Instead the group can be helped to weigh the criticism by considering its merits as well as its deficiencies. After doing so, the group can then decide whether to ignore, respond, explain, or incorporate the criticism into their future actions.

Who Should Facilitate?

We have emphasized the importance of having a knowledgeable and skillful facilitator working with a school when enacting changes. But who should be the facilitator?

We have struggled with this question for many years and still struggle with it. Some of the facilitators who have been used with League schools are persons within the school (school counselors, school teachers, building administrators), within the district (supervisors), consultants outside the district, and university faculty members. In the future, we plan to try a new model of facilitation--the use of practitioners from an "experienced" school to work with a new school. We are particularly intrigued about school-to-school work because it promises reciprocal benefits.

There are advantages and disadvantages of placing facilitator responsibility with any particular role. For example, an outside consultant or university person can remain apart from the inner politics of the school and thus help the group reason according to more abstract principles. On the other hand, a district supervisor will be aware of inner politics, the distribution of resources, and the operation of the informal system and will be able to use this knowledge to expedite matters.

A principal assuming the role of group facilitator has the same advantage of knowing the informal system but has the disadvantage of being seen as manipulating the group process to arrive at decisions he or she would prefer. A teacher as group facilitator must walk a delicate balancing act in assuming this role while maintaining day-to-day personal relations with peers in the school.

School counselors and assistant principals have the advantage of being in a brokering position (between students, teachers, parents, and administrators). School counselors are more likely to have the formal preparation in communication and group skills and are accustomed to acting as mediators in group situations. Often they are seen as too far outside the mainstream, however, to appreciate the unique problems of teachers (even though they have most likely been classroom teachers themselves).

Assistant principals, on the other hand, are likely to have been trained in group dynamics and leadership theory but from a management orientation. They are likely to have information about school-wide issues and are more likely to be seen as having greater power to implement decisions once made.

Whether counselors or administrators in such a position can exercise group process skills and stay removed from the power influences of their superiors is a concern that should be seriously considered. Ultimately, after discussing the issue, the decision should be the school's to determine.

We, the university staff of the Program for School Improvement, offer a basic menu of facilitation opportunities that we believe to be the "floor" (not the "ceiling") for most schools. We meet for at least a day every three months with a core of at least four members from each school (the principal, two teachers, and another person of the school's choice such as another teacher, parent, or district representative). These meetings involve 10 or more schools at a time and are held at regional or central sites.

During those meetings, we spend several hours working with actual facilitation concerns and encouraging schools to network with each other on mutual problems. Additionally, we provide a 60- to 90-minute breakout session on facilitation skills, covering such topics as dealing with dysfunctional members, conflict resolution, building cohesion, and observing/intervening in group roadblocks. At the end of the day, each team takes an hour to consolidate its learnings into a plan of immediate actions to take back to its school.

The university has an on-site facilitator for each school who visits for a full day in the winter. The facilitator interviews principal, teachers, and students; reviews the school plan; and participates in discussions with the school's team. The university facilitator summarizes his or her observations in a writ-

> **Empowered schools have an opportunity to rethink the conventions of the school. Curriculum, scheduling, grouping, and grading are all potential topics for discussion.**

ten report to the school.

Furthermore, we hold a three-day summer facilitation institute at a mountain retreat for the principal and key teachers who wish to (a) refine their own internal skills to support their school's decision-making process and (b) serve as members of a cadre of experienced facilitators who can help new schools during the next school year.

We also help individual school teams identify facilitation needs they have for the coming year, in addition to those services provided by the League of Professional School activities. If they need more frequent external help, we provide them with a list of other practitioners in their community, district, regional educational service agency, and the state.

We believe that the staff development of internal facilitators within a school and the network of practitioner-to-practitioner facilitation across schools is our best hope for providing facilitation to over 40 schools.

Conclusion

Staff developers working with a district which is making similar site-based, shared-governance changes may find useful our insights into the complexities of school change and the role of facilitation. A staff development plan extending over many years should be developed to assist schools in providing their own internal facilitation.

The need is apparent, the potential results for improving schools and educating students is enormous, and the complexities are great

Acknowledgement

The Program for School Improvement and The League of Professional Schools is sponsored by The University of Georgia, BellSouth Foundation, the Georgia Leadership Academy, and the National Diffusion Network of the United States Department of Education. This article represents the opinion of the authors. It carries no official endorsement by our sponsors. Furthermore, we wish to thank Barbara Lunsford for her helpful suggestions.

References

Bion, W. (1959). *Experience in groups.* New York: Basic Books.

Brookover, W., Beady, C., Flood, P., Schweiter, J., & Wisenbaker, J. (1979). *School social systems and students' achievement: Schools can make a difference.* New York: Praeger.

Dewey, J. (1916). *Democracy and education.* New York: Macmillan.

Glickman, C.D. (1987). Unlocking school reform: Uncertainty as a condition of professionalism. *Phi Delta Kappan, 68*(10), 120-122.

Glickman, C.D. (1990). Pushing school reform to a new edge: The ironies of school empowerment. *Phi Delta Kappan, 72*(1), 68-75.

Hall, G.E., & Hord, S.M. (1987). *Change in schools: Facilitating the process.* New York: State University of New York Press.

Hayes, R. (In press). Group work and the teaching of ethics. *Journal for Specialists in Group Work.*

Johnson, D.W., & Johnson, R.T. (1987). *Joining together: Group theory and group skills* (3rd ed.). Englewood Cliffs, NJ: Prentice-Hall.

Pfeiffer, J., Goodstein, L., & Nolan, T. (1989). *Shaping strategic planning.* Glenview, IL: Scott, Foresman and Company.

Reid, W.A. (1987). Institutions and practice: Professional education reports and the language of reform. *Educational Researcher, 16*(8), 10-15.

Tuckman, B., & Jensen, M. (1977). Stages of small-group development revisited. *Group and Organizational Studies, 2,* 419-427.

Ward, N. (1989). *Case study: A high school faculty develops collegiality around the knowledge base on teaching and learning.* Paper presented at the annual meeting of the American Educational Research Association, San Francisco, CA.

Wolfe, R. (1969). A model for curriculum evaluation. *Psychology in the Schools,* (6), 107-108.

Yalom, I. (1985). *The theory and practice of group psychotherapy* (3rd ed.). New York: Basic Books.

About the Authors

Margery B. Ginsberg is an educational researcher, author, and consultant in Boulder, Colorado. She has worked with several states on federal program initiatives and served as the Texas Title I technical assistance contact for the United States Department of Education. Dr. Ginsberg currently serves as a consultant for statewide systems of school support. Her work is informed by teaching experience on two Indian reservations and college teaching in the areas of multicultural education, evaluation, and assessment. In addition to publishing numerous articles, she is co-author, with Raymond Wlodkowski, of *Diversity and Motivation: Culturally Responsive Teaching* (Jossey-Bass, 1995). Ginsberg can be reached at 6033 Jay Rd., Boulder, CO 80301. Telephone: (303) 530-4182. Fax: (303) 581-9518. e-mail: margery@edlink.com

Joseph F. Johnson Jr. is the Director of School Improvement Initiatives at the Charles A. Dana Center at the University of Texas at Austin. He serves as co-director of the U.S. Department of Education's Region VIII Comprehensive Center, the STAR (Support for Texas Academic Renewal) Center, and the director of several other research and technical assistance efforts focused on improving the effectiveness of schools in poor communities. Recently, Dr. Johnson served as the state director of Title I and several other federal and state education programs at the Texas Education Agency. He can be reached at the Charles A. Dana Center, University of Texas at Austin, 2901 North IH-35, Suite 2.200, Austin, TX 78722-2348. Telephone: 512-475-9708. e-mail: jfjohnson@mail.utexas.edu

Cerylle A. Moffett is an independent consultant who specializes in facilitating educational change; interactive designs for the training of trainers; and developing curriculum, instruction, and assessment systems that integrate curriculum content standards and complex reasoning skills. A member of ASCD's Professional Development staff for 15 years, Moffett

151

most recently served as ASCD program manager for professional development. She is co-author of ASCD's Dimensions of Learning program and was project coordinator of Assisting Change in Education (ACE), a research-based facilitation and consultation skills training program for organization development specialists and school improvement facilitators. Moffett has designed and delivered staff development programs for educators across the United States and Canada, and for the Department of Defense Dependent Schools in Panama and the Far East. She is dedicated to creating responsive adult learning communities in the public and private sectors, and to facilitating substantive change in the quality of teaching and learning at all levels.

She can be reached at Cerylle Moffett & Associates, 916 De Wolfe Dr., Alexandria, VA 22308. Telephone: (703) 780-6502. Fax: (703) 780-9192. e-mail: CERYLLE@ AOL.COM